WINDOWS ON LIFE

WINDOWS ON LIFE

BY

CARL HEATH KOPF

"Window, let day in, and let life out."
—ROMEO AND JULIET

Essay Index Reprint Series

BX
7233
K83

ESSAY INDEX

106690

BOOKS FOR LIBRARIES PRESS
FREEPORT, NEW YORK

STANDARD BOOK NUMBER:
8369-1041-9

LIBRARY OF CONGRESS CATALOG CARD NUMBER:
70-76908

PRINTED IN THE UNITED STATES OF AMERICA

To

THE MOUNT VERNON CHURCH OF BOSTON

This book is my gift of labor and love on her 100th birthday in 1942, because of her patience with my ministry and because she has loaned me a Window on Beacon Street, to look through and to dream through.

C. H. K.

PREFACE IN BRIEF

My only excuse for letting these informal papers be printed is that my heart is in them. They are what I like to do, more personal by intention than philosophic or sermonic. These parables and essays are written primarily for the people who think they have lost interest in religion, in the hope that ancient truth may answer some of our modern questions.

Let me thank the people of the Mount Vernon Church of Boston who have granted me a quiet study with windows on life and without a telephone.

And to the officers of the Columbia Broadcasting System in Boston I owe great thanks because of their encouragement in our program, "From a Window on Beacon Street."

Herrick House,   CARL HEATH KOPF
Boston.

CONTENTS

WINDOWS ON LIFE

NEARSIGHTED OR FARSIGHTED?

WHAT would we do without windows? Windows to let the heart out as well as windows to let the light in.

A window to dream through is almost a necessity for every living soul. Yours may look out on the familiar street scene with the familiar friends and enemies passing in endless procession.

Or your window may span an arch of sky and frame a woodland. Or it may give boundaries to your own handwrought garden, the result of years of care. Thank God for windows!

Not having them, we should miss them more than we know. The most fervent request I can remember came from the lips of a prisoner walled within a gloomy jail who answered, when ˉ asked if I could bring him anything, "I wish you could bring me a window to see the springtime beyond the high wall."

And who of υ will ever forget the window we have wakened toward to catch an augury of the kind of day ahead? If we glimpse the sparkling of the sun on the opposite wall, or in the trees beyond, we rejoice for a fair day. If the wall is dull, the leaves lack-lustre or whipping in a gale, or if snow has fallen in the night we read the message in all its quick clarity—

through a window. In one sense a window is like a good friend; it minimizes its own presence, except when it is befouled, and brings us impressions of better things outside of itself that we should make our own.

It is my good fortune to have two windows looking out upon the world from my study. I should perhaps say misfortune, for such windows often keep me from full concentration upon my theological and homiletical studies. I must confess that I have even known the Bible to rest before me almost unread while I have become absorbed in the plodding patience of an old man selling violets on the street below. If this is heresy I am sorry. I have thought of frosting my windows, but I think the frost would creep down the window sill and over the floor, up the legs of my chair and into my heart.

The window to my left in my study looks out on traffic-bewildered, apartment-house-hedged Beacon Street. Another window to my right frames the wide Charles River and the vast, classical façade of the Massachusetts Institute of Technology almost a mile away in Cambridge.

When I open my window on Beacon Street, the stream of consciousness beats an incessant tattoo, day and night, horns bleating like Paris taxicabs. From early afternoon to late evening newsboys shout their scare-headlines. Street cars on the counter-crossing, Massachusetts Avenue, occasional crashes in the midnight hours when the traffic lights are out, and the fools are too, all this adds up to great unlikelihood that grass will grow in Beacon Street.

I see sad things. The halt, the lame and the blind tramp in steady procession through the doors of the doctors' office building across the street. They come with hope in their faces, from Newton and Charlestown, Brookline and Chelsea. They want healing.

Now a street car stops at the far corner, a woman steps down, then turns and reaches up to take her twelve-year-old son in her arms. He is surely heavier than his mother. She carries her crippled son over the piece of street, then up the curb, over the sidewalk and into the house of the physician. My morning's study is spoiled. With something on my heart it is hard to get something on my mind.

I want to see what is going on in that street, for on the average I see the same things that happen on the Champs Elysées in Paris or on Main Street in Wichita. But I do not get so many books read, for looking, nor do I polish my sermons so you can see your face in them.

When the noise of Beacon Street gets too nerve-racking, I turn to the quiet calm of my window overlooking the river. White sails, shadows on the pillars of M. I. T., the long-range view, neat perfection of line and color, these give me antidote for Beacon Street.

I cannot decide which window I like the better. I know I need both. Because if I spend too much time looking at the close-ups of life on Beacon Street I develop a bad case of myopia, nearsightedness. Things right here at the end of my nose will loom gigantic and seem more important than they really are. The optometrists say we Americans are gradually becoming a nearsighted people from lack of far horizons and the long look.

And if I spend all my time day-dreaming out through my far-away window on the Charles River side I shall be in danger of hyperopia, farsightedness, seeing things at a distance but missing the practical realities close around me.

When a man tells you he knows exactly how to solve the problems of Central Europe and then confesses that he forgot to vote last Election Day at the polling place around the corner, you have met a bad case of hyperopia.

The obvious truth is that more people are afflicted with myopia and hyperopia than ever go to the oculist. They probably do not know they have either disease, because it is more subtle, yet more dangerous, in the soul than in the optic system.

When you meet a charming sinner who sums up his profound philosophy of life by chanting, having heard it somewhere before, "Eat, drink and be merry, for tomorrow we die," you have met a victim of myopia, nearsightedness.

For the truth is he probably will not die tomorrow, unless he drinks cyanide today. The chances are about 10,000 to 1 that he will go on living tomorrow and the next day, living with himself, his body, his conscience, living with his family, his friends and his job, if he keeps it. And he will go on living with his God.

And what does myopia like that lead to? Paul Dunbar has answered:

> This is the debt I pay
> Just for one riotous day,——
> Years of regret and grief,
> Sorrow without relief.
>
> Slight was the thing I bought,
> Small was the debt I thought,
> Poor was the loan at best——
> God! but the interest! [1]

Some of us pay a high price for our myopia, because we refuse to see as far ahead as the middle of next week, let alone next year.

The only cure for a bad case of myopia is to develop a little farsightedness to match the nearsightedness.

My friend, Edgar Pray, teaches high school near Boston. One morning he asked his students to write out on a note any special requests for seat locations. One boy wrote, "Please, I would like a back seat, because I am farsighted." Knowing the devilish inclinations of this particular lad, Mr. Pray wrote this comment upon his request, "Granted, that you are far-sighted in more ways than one."

[1] Printed by permission of Dodd, Mead & Co.

It is nearsighted to sacrifice tomorrow's health for today's gluttony.

It is nearsighted to believe that because something looks hopeless today, life will always be hopeless.

It is farsighted to live for heaven after death and not bother about a little bit of heaven on earth, now.

It is hyperopic to dream about what we would do with our lives if we had a big chance, while we miss the little chances lying all about us unseen in our blindness.

It is farsighted, too farsighted, to think only about what might have been or will be, and not make use of what is.

This balancing of emphasis upon things near and far, temporal and eternal, real and abstract, fact and theory, is the most delicate of problems. And no one sees things in right perspective until he attains some right relation between foreground and background.

On the whole, background is more important than we ever guess. An apprentice to a famous artist suggested to his master, "Perhaps I could help you by painting in the background of your next picture."

"Ah, no," contradicted the artist, "you may do the foreground, I shall do the background."

The background is that important.

A doctor's skill for ten minutes in the operating room is the foreground. But at least seven years of college, medical school, interneship, these are the background.

A preacher's twenty minutes in the pulpit is the

foreground. But hours of meditation on the deep things of life, these hours are the background.

The more powerful a life is to be, the more that life must be built on a long plan.

You must steer a great ship a mile ahead. The laws of momentum make that inevitable.

The *Titanic* sank in 1912 because she was going too fast for the distance her steersman could see ahead in the darkness of the North Atlantic night.

The irony of it all is that the *Titanic* was believed unsinkable because of her separate, airtight compartments. But the Unsinkable Ship was sinking. The passengers would not believe it. Hundreds refused to get into the lifeboats.

In spite of the tragedy of it all, the survivors remember most vividly the pink glow of the sunrise the next morning as the light bathed the innocent looking icebergs standing about in the sea. Lifeboats with the few living souls intermingled with the bergs and near-by stood the *Carpathia,* the rescue ship, which had taken terrific risks in coming through the ice fields at full speed, all through the night, to be near the disaster.

Hundreds were lost, only a few saved, that dark, moonless night in April, 1912.

Why were they lost? Because the *Titanic,* anxious to set a record on her maiden crossing, was speeding faster than she could see ahead. A ship that size must be steered a mile ahead and that night she could not see half that distance.

So with a ship of state or with one's personal life. It must be steered a mile ahead. We had better be that farsighted.

Most of the personal and public tragedies of this world, from your failure to pass that examination because you were not prepared, to the fall of the Roman Empire because that Empire was not prepared to endure, can be written down as caused by either myopia or hyperopia, nearsightedness, or farsightedness.

The high purpose of wise education and vital religion is to give us clear vision, both near and far, without which the people perish.

YOU WOULDN'T TREAT A
WHEELBARROW THAT WAY

THE smallest shop I know is a watch repairing cubbyhole where the skilled craftsman has been in business for the last forty years. The shop is four feet wide
and twelve feet long with enough space in the middle
for only two customers.

The walls are covered with clocks; grandfather
clocks, banjo clocks, alarm clocks, cuckoo clocks and
kitchen clocks. And when Walter Austin times a
timepiece, he takes his time so that by the time you
have time to come back for your timepiece he has
timed it to the right time. Any weekday you will see
him bent over his bench facing his little front window,
eyepiece focussed on a tiny hairspring and tweezers
doing his delicate bidding. I had passed him a hundred times without stopping.

But my turn came. Suddenly I began being late for
meetings I should have been on time for. My fine
watch was slowing down.

Just as your watch is precious to you mine is precious to me, a gift from my mother and father at the
romantic age of *wenty-one, supposedly old enough
to take care of a good watch. But I had grown care-

9

less. I assumed that a watch would run almost forever if I wound it once a day. I quickly became conscious of my mistake.

Walter Austin took the piece tenderly, held it in
the palm of his hand and listened attentively to my
complaint, "This watch seems to be running down
but I don't know why because I've never had any
trouble with it."

"When did you last have it cleaned and oiled?"
Austin asked me, and I fumbled for the answer.

"Didn't I bring it in just last year, or the year before?" I hinted, hoping Walter Austin would absolve
my sin. But he gave me no comfort.

"You haven't given me this watch for a check-up
in the last five years," he intoned, and I felt the coming judgment.

"You wouldn't treat a wheelbarrow that way!" he
added. I hung my head in shame and took my punishment in silence, as befits the guilty, for I had been
very careless with something very precious.

He saw how hard I was taking it, so his voice soft-
ened a little, as he explained, "Your watch has 15-
jewelled bearings which gather dust and grit and
need to be cleaned at least every two years and have
a very tiny drop of oil to keep them running
smoothly. You wouldn't treat a wheelbarrow that
way because a wheelbarrow would squeak. But your
watch keeps quiet. It just runs behind."

I begged Walter Austin's pardon, for he took my
insult to my own watch quite personally. I begged

the watch's pardon and I left it for a careful grooming.

But I have not slept well since, for even in my dreams I seem to hear the echoing ring of that clear judgment, "You wouldn't treat a wheelbarrow that way."

For if a man should take care of his watch, how much more should he take care of some other things, infinitely more precious.

Sometimes a man treats his body worse than he treats his wheelbarrow. He over-eats, he over-drinks, he over-smokes. Then he under-exercises, under-sleeps. Soon his body runs behind, like my uncared-for watch.

I do not mean to say that all the illness in the world is caused by someone's carelessness with this human body, the temple of the spirit. I know how often hereditary weakness, accident, or just sheer hard luck causes innocent suffering. But after these exceptions are granted it is still a more general rule than we like to admit that much—perhaps 90 per cent—of the illness in the world could be prevented if we all used uncommon good sense about our diet and daily conduct.

We know full well we ought to check minor symptoms before they turn into major operations. We know it but we do not do it.

We know in theory the simple principles of dietary health but we do not practise them. A wheelbarrow would squeak if it were treated that way, over-loaded and under-cared-for, but our bodies suffer in silence and just run down, and finally out.

Sometimes a man treats his brain the way he would never treat a wheelbarrow, and offhand it would seem that a brain might be as important to its owner as his watch. Like the wheelbarrow, the brain will break down if it is over-loaded or it will rust if unused. Over-loaded with worry or fear the brain suffers impossible tension and possible breakdown. Under-loaded, living with nothing on one's mind, leads to intellectual apathy which is not far from spiritual death.

I have referred to worry and fear as the two chief causes of an over-loaded mind. And both of these could be conquered with a little will. "Worry is interest paid on trouble before it comes due," is Dean Inge's way of saying what Mark Twain put more humorously, "I have had a great many troubles in my life, most of which never happened." Not only is it possible that the things we worry about may never happen, but if they do happen they may do us good. Often what seems like bad luck turns out to be good luck. Lin Yutang tells the story of a Chinese nobleman who lost a beautiful horse. This was bad luck, so his friends came to console him on his misfortune. But the next day the lost horse returned with ten other fine wild horses which he had befriended in the wilderness. This was good luck, so the nobleman's friends gathered to congratulate him upon his fine fortune. But the next day, while trying to break one of the wild horses to the saddle, the nobleman's son was thrown and his leg broken. Bad luck; so the friends gathered to bemoan the nobleman's tragedy. But on the following day a local war was declared and the nobleman's son was unable to fight in the bloody battle because of his broken leg. It turns out later he would certainly have been killed. So the nobleman's friends gather for a final feast of rejoicing over the quick turn back to good luck. Bad luck, good luck, bad luck, good luck, such is the turn of the wheel. But who knows which is which? If a fortune falls in your lap your troubles begin. If you lose your money you may begin to find your soul. If you are homely you have to depend on character, and if you are too beautiful you have a hard time keeping your character. Is there any good luck which may not be very bad luck with the right chain of sequence? Is there any bad luck which may not turn out to be good luck somewhere, sometime?

The one thing we can be sure of is this. Whatever happens to a strong man or woman will be good luck, somehow.

But if worry wounds its thousands, fear kills its tens of thousands. There is nothing in earth or heaven or hell we have any right to be afraid of, except the possibility of our own personal failure. Nothing else in the wide universe can hurt us inwardly, which is the only direction that counts over the years. God gives us so much capacity, a set of human situations, a few chances and many choices to do good or ill. Our only fear should be that we may fail to live up to our capacity, miss the few chances and make the wrong choices. And there is no need to be panicky about that, because it is the one thing in the world we can do most about. We may not be able to alter the price of wheat on the Chicago Market but we can alter the direction of our personal conduct.

Perhaps even worse than the worry-ridden and the fear-possessed are the empty-headed. These are they who stop studying the day they bow gracefully and accept the sheepskin, thereupon hiding it in the attic trunk. It is sad beyond describing when a man or woman closes the mind on any subject and refuses to listen to or read any new evidence, learn a new hobby, explore a hitherto unknown field of study or search out the answer to a serious question. No one anywhere in a day of correspondence schools, radio education, free lectures, has any excuse for not keeping mentally awake. In and around any great city in any given year there are taught, for adults beyond school age, many courses on subjects all the way from astronomy to zoology. And many of these are given free under government auspices, the others at very small cost. Hardly a day goes by without a free lecture or concert at your public library or some other cultural center. The only cost is the carfare and the gumption. And more people have the carfare than have the gumption. They would never treat a wheelbarrow the way they are treating their brains because a wheelbarrow would squeak, but their brains run down, silently.

Then look at the way some of us treat our jobs, cutting corners in the morning, at lunch and at five o'clock, doing only enough work to get by with the boss. I hear someone complain, "If only I had a job with a future I could make good." But every job has a future. If Edison could start by selling papers and Dr. Cadman could start as a breaker boy in the coal mines of England, you and I can start anywhere we see and work in the only direction there is, up.

An artist on government relief can paint every bit as glorious a picture as an artist in his Beacon Hill studio, if the glorious painting is within him, waiting to work out.

And sometimes a husband or a wife treats the family somewhat worse than a wheelbarrow would be treated. Somewhere there is a man who gives his wife a few left-over scraps of affection. His first love is the cash register down town or the club out in the suburbs. He has grown out of romanticism and hates sentimental things. Once he was very sentimental, when the competition for her was keener than it is now long after the wedding bells. He has no time for a second honeymoon taking her away from the dishes and the vacuum cleaner.

Or perchance it is the once adoring wife who now puts all her adoration into bridge and shopping and gives her husband the feeling that at last he is only a glorified meal ticket. You would never treat a wheelbarrow that way.

And parents too sometimes treat their children the way they would not treat a wheelbarrow. Not long ago a busy father called on the dean of freshmen at an American college and declared, "My son has just enrolled and I hope you can keep an eye on him. My business has kept me away from home and, frankly, I don't seem to understand the boy. I hope you'll take a hand and straighten him out." The dean turned squarely around in his swivel chair, gave this clear ultimatum, "Sir, if you don't understand your son after nineteen years of being his father, I refuse to do in four years the job you should have done long ago." Such a father is only one grade above the famous member of the English House of Lords who one day in Hyde Park met one of his own children playing and observed, "By Jove, child, I've seen you before somewhere!"

You would never treat a wheelbarrow that way.

DETOUR

"DETOUR!" How that sign can take the fun out of a cross country motor tour or a Sunday afternoon's ride. There you are sailing along in your fine car over the smooth concrete when suddenly someone in the back seat chirps up with, "Oh, oh, don't look now, but that sign ahead has bad news written all over it."

"Detour!" Everybody groans and you shift into second gear and the jouncy buggy ride begins over the back country lanes.

We can sympathize with the visitor to America who remarked that he liked the roads made by that Scotchman Macadam but he did not think much of the roads built by that Frenchman Detour.

We were driving hummingly up through the Blue Grass country of Kentucky, where the pasture land is flecked with grazing thoroughbred racing horses and their dancing colts. On our way home after nine thousand miles of cross country driving we blessed our good luck in having met so few detours. But we spoke too soon. Suddenly all the cars passing us in the opposite direction seemed to be covered with mud.

Over the next rise and around two turns, there

hung a sign as big as a barn door. "Detour." And there was no dodging it. "Detour, fifty-six miles." I cannot tell you what that sign did to my blood pressure or to my decorous language.

We had to take that detour. In we plunged with our nice shiny car, right into the middle of a sea of mud. A cloudburst had fallen the night before. We slithered and slipped from hub cap to fender. We bounced from the floor to the roof. We waited for a load of hay to pass and then got stalled behind a mired bus.

But just as things were at their worst we came out at a country cross roads where the sign said, "Detour, by way of Hodgenville."

"Hodgenville"—that sounds familiar. Hodgenville, Kentucky. A log cabin, Abraham Lincoln's birthplace! Detour by way of Hodgenville. Why, that's good news, that's not bad news. My blood pressure calmed down, my language improved. Instead of cursing our luck we began to bless it, that we had been forced to take a detour, by way of Hodgenville.

It is even now just a small Kentucky village, with a rickety country store where loafers sit around the cracker barrel telling stories of all colors and settling the world's problems, just as they did that winter evening in 1809 when one of the old timers observed, "I see they got a new baby today over to Tom and Nancy Lincoln's cabin. He's the homeliest critter I ever laid eyes on."

One never knows in how small a village greatness will be born. Who ever heard of Dole, France, until Louis Pasteur was born there? Why would anybody ever remember Bridges Creek, Virginia? Because George Washington was born there. What claim has little Domremy, France, to a place in history? Only that Joan of Arc saw the light of day there. And what shall we say of Bethlehem, the smallest town with the biggest meaning in the history of the world? So take heart if you were born in a place so small almost nobody ever heard of it. They may hear of it because *you* do something worth remembering.

But let me get back to this detour, by way of Hodgenville. As we drove into the park marked "Lincoln's birthplace" we looked in vain for the rustic cabin. All we could see was a handsome marble Greek style edifice. Then we discovered that the most famous log cabin in the world has been surrounded by this marble shelter so that rain and vandals may not damage the precious one-room house with its huge fireplace and its stalwart walls. I wonder if Tom Lincoln was as shiftless as some historians make out? That log cabin was well designed, well put together. Maybe he was a better father than we have commonly supposed. A guard stood watch beside the cabin and a little sign at the door said "Please do not enter." The cabin was already full, with an invisible presence. A glory shone round the place and within. It seemed almost like hallowed ground.

Detour, by way of Hodgenville. In spite of the mud, that detour is one of the best roads I have ever taken.

The surest thing we know about this, our common life, is that sooner or later each of us will come up to that sign with big black letters that cannot be denied, "Detour." What will happen then, is the question. Will we curse God and our bad luck or will we make something out of it and go "by way of Hodgenville"?

Some of you know what I am talking about. You were sailing along on the high road of economic independence at sixty miles an hour, the road straight ahead as far as you could see. Money in your pockets, a song on your lips, time to eat, drink and be merry. Then you came around a curve and Whoa! Detour! In a few minutes a stock ticker put the brakes on you, you lost that good job. Overnight you had to move from Fifth Avenue to Canal Street, across the railroad tracks. How did you take it? Cry like a baby or straighten up like a man with a backbone and make a new beginning right down in the mud and scum of things? You know what you did. Some of you sang a song in the night and kept that little family together around a WPA check instead of a box full of clipped coupons. Poorer in the purse by several dollar signs, somebody today is richer in the deep places of the heart and soul where God sees. He is on a detour, by way of Hodgenville.

Somebody else was yesterday sailing easily along on the highway of good health—strong, eager, full of the joy of living. Then last night you met your detour sign. Was it an accident that broke your bones and put you to bed for a year? Was it infantile paralysis striking at you like lightning? Was it a long hidden malignancy finally choking your blood stream? It happens every moment of every day, somewhere. How are you taking that detour?

Somebody else has been riding the high road of a good reputation and personal success. Everybody thought well of you, and your friends stood by you and were proud to know you. But suddenly you made a mistake, you cut across the current of public opinion. Then right in the center of your highroad you saw that sign, "Detour," and you began to have to take the bumps. Social ostracism, public ridicule, perchance off to prison you must go, rightly or wrongly. What will that detour do to your spirit? Make it or break it? Will it be the end or the beginning of your life? To every man or woman in prison today, and to their families, I say that even that detour can be "by way of Hodgenville."

And now I see some of you on the high road of a good education, college career planned, choice of vocation made. The lights were all green until your father died without insurance and you came up against it, "Detour."

So you have chucked the school books into the closet for a while and have taken any job you could find to keep that little family together. How are you doing? Are you suffering through a miserable detour or are you on a detour, by way of Hodgenville? I hope I know your answer. Working every day you can still burn the midnight light bulb to try to keep up your intellectual vigor. You will not be so far behind when you get around that detour because you will go by way of Hodgenville. Thomas Edison, tweaking a telegraph key by day and experimenting with test tubes and batteries half the night, made the best of his detour and it became a through highway. Gutenberg, fooling with movable type after hours in the back room of his little jewelry shop in Mainz, made his detour count for something better than the main road. I suppose one of the high tests of our personal living is not how fast we can travel on the straightaway but how we take the forced detours.

The last detour I see is that sad one around a broken love affair. Both of you were meant for each other; you had the diamond on your finger, the day all set with the parson. Then you had to put it off; family objections, economic impossibilities. That is your detour. Or worse, you lost the dearest one on earth to you. The detour seems impassable. But mark this, somewhere along your detour you will meet a man or a woman, a little child, who is starved for the love you have to give. And if, instead of jumping off the bridge, you will answer that loneliness you see, even that detour can be by way of Hodgenville and you will be happier than you had thought possible.

THE ISLES OF SHOALS

For millions of Americans the Isles of Shoals are nothing but a grim reminder of tragedy under the sea, the graveyard of submarines. For a few hundreds of Americans the Isles of Shoals are the most off-the-beaten-path summer refuge in America. Like the rocky peaks of half a dozen mighty mountains rising out of the sea, these islands, seven miles off the mainland near Portsmouth, New Hampshire, have never known a traffic light nor a train whistle. Quietness, ad infinitum, is the ancient rule except when the fog horn on White Island booms out its deep warning for three seconds, then is off for twenty-seven seconds.

Hardly a tree has been able to grow against the wind on these rocky cliffs but, even so, there is a mystic, indefinable attraction, not unlike the spell cast by the moors of Southern England, a spell of wonder and power in elemental things. If you have never been to the Shoals you cannot understand why anyone would want to go. If you have been there you cannot understand why anyone should fail to go.

What do we do out there, with no roads or golf courses or wild forests? There is good food served in a huge, well-managed hotel. Then there is always a glorious view of rolling ocean, breaking surf, incoming and outgoing sailing ships, for the harbor at Gosport is a much sought haven in the time of storm. Rolling lawns carefully seeded over the rocks make croquet grounds and badminton courts. There is tennis on two courts and, preferred above all else, climbing and resting on the rocks to seaward as the breakers toss and spray from out the wide ocean. Conferences on religion and life are held during the summer in the little chapel, where the candlelight service at eventime is the most winsome ritual I know, with worshippers climbing the hill, each carrying a candle. After the candles are hung in the chapel a short service of prayer and reading closes the day and sleep is deep with rest while shafts of light from the lighthouse move in protecting circles over your head. The prayer which closes each evening's meditation is this:

In the holy quiet of this hour let us draw near to Him who heareth prayer. And let us remember that He listeneth more to our hearts than to our words. Let each of us bring an offering of penitence, if not of purity; of love, if not of holiness; of teachableness, if not of wisdom; and let us beseech Him by His Holy Spirit to bring down an answer of peace to our souls.

The swimming off the diving raft is cool and sparkling. The only exciting event of the day is the arrival of the steamer from Portsmouth.

Two of the islands, Appledore and Smutty Nose, offer an amazing contrast in beauty and ugliness.

Appledore! The name is as full of sweetness and light as the name Smutty Nose is full of sourness and dark.

The geography of the two islands bears out this contrast. Appledore, the largest of the island group, about a half mile long, named after a Devonshire village, is well rounded, high and covered with vegetation. Huckleberry, bayberry bushes, elder, sumach, woodbine, wild cherry and shadbush.

There are at least six varieties of lovely ferns on Appledore. At the first breath of October the slopes are afire with the crimson huckleberry. On the highest point a clean white coast guard station nestles snugly beneath the always briskly waving Stars and Stripes.

But Smutty Nose is a much smaller island, low, flat and unlovely, with little grass to cover its bare, broken rocks; and a south-eastern point which dips into the ocean, covered with black seaweed, gives the appearance of a smutty nose. Hence the unlovely name. About the only vegetation is the poisonous henbane, an herb of the nightshade family.

And the history of Appledore and Smutty Nose is just as amazing a contrast as the names and the geography. On Appledore was the homestead of Celia Laighton Thaxter, poet, friend of the poets, historian, chronicler of the Shoals. The Laighton family has been a legend at the Shoals for almost a hundred years. It was about 1840 that Celia's father was defeated for Governor of New Hampshire and then eschewed all human society by becoming light keeper at White Island where Oscar Laighton lived until he was sixteen before he even visited Portsmouth and saw his first horse. Oscar died in 1939, within a few weeks of his hundredth birthday. So Appledore Island has twined about its rocky inlets the poetry of Celia Thaxter, "Good-bye Sweet Day," written on the evening of her engagement day, to Mr. Thaxter; "The Sunrise Never Failed Us Yet," "The Sandpiper."

And besides cultivating her poetry and her colorful flowers grown almost out of the rocks on Appledore, Celia Thaxter had time to cultivate friendships with Hawthorne, Whittier, President Pierce, who came far out to her island crag to rest in her father's hotel and to become aware of her beauty and her poetry. That a woman living so much away from the world could so well understand the world is another testimony to what we all have sometimes guessed, that once in a while somebody off the mainland of life's confusion can interpret that very confusion with more clarity than those at the center of the vortex. It is not always so, but it is sometimes so.

The history of Smutty Nose is not so lovely. Witness the "Murder at Smutty Nose," so clearly described in all its horror by Edmund Pearson in his book of the same title. So close to Appledore that a man might throw a stone across the channel, Smutty Nose has blood stains on its rocks that will never rub off as long as horror stories are read and somehow enjoyed. Louis Wagner was the villain and it happened on the moonlit, cold night of March 5, 1873. The only house on Smutty Nose was owned by John Hontvet, fisherman, who lived there with his wife, Maren, and had come from Norway five years before. Living with the Hontvets were Maren's sister, Karen, and Matthew Hontvet and Ivan Christensen with his lovely bride, Anethe, who was, "fair and merry, with thick bright sunny hair, which was so long it reached, when unbraided, nearly to her knees; blue-eyed, with brilliant teeth and clear, fresh complexion, beautiful and beloved beyond expression by her young husband."

Louis Wagner had helped the men with their fishing in the waters around the Shoals and had lived with the Hontvets for a few weeks. He was a rosy-faced Prussian, big and strong, twenty-eight years old.

On the evening of the 5th of March Wagner saw the three men of Hontvet's household in Portsmouth where they had sailed their *Clara Bella* with a load of fish and where they mentioned to Wagner that they would have to stay in Portsmouth overnight to meet a train bringing necessary bait from Boston.

Wagner had failed as a fisherman and on this particular night owed two weeks' board in Portsmouth and had no work in sight. The devil found work, dirty work, for his idle hands.

Stealing a dory at the dock-front, Wagner rowed ten miles out to Smutty Nose, where he knew the three women must be alone, entered the house by moonlight to look for money which he knew Hontvet had saved. The three women, wakened by the intruder, were savagely attacked before they knew what it was all about. Karen and the lovely Anethe were killed. Maren escaped the bloody axe by hiding in a cave near the water's edge until dawn, when she called help from Appledore. The men of the family, returning from Portsmouth, gasped in terror at the carnage, then sailed back to Portsmouth to spread the alarm, for Maren had seen Wagner in the moonlight clearly enough to have no possible doubt as to the murderer's identity.

Wagner had rowed back to the mainland in the early morning hours and taken a train to Boston where he was arrested later in the day and, after trial and conviction, was sentenced and hung by the neck until dead. For all the blood on his hands and soul he had found only about twenty dollars in the house of the Hontvets. Rather cheap murder, and double murder at that.

Such is the history of Smutty Nose.

There is another Appledore and another Smutty Nose. They are not at the Isles of Shoals but within the potential character of each human person. Some of us live on Appledore, some of us live on Smutty Nose. Some souls take the high way and some take the low. Dr. Jekyll and Mr. Hyde is more than a work of fiction, it is something each of us knows something about in the place where we make our decisions and thereafter our character.

And these two possibilities are set as close together within us as Appledore and Smutty Nose are at the Shoals. When we live with good books and fine hopes and gracious memories we live on Appledore. When we live with tawdry reading and foul intentions and seared consciences we live on Smutty Nose. That is the question and it is the principal question of all our days, Where do we live, on Appledore or Smutty Nose?

LOST AND FOUND

WHAT they are not holding in the cupboards of the street car company's lost and found office has probably never been lost. Hundreds of umbrellas, in all colors of the spectrum, with handles of ivory and bone and jade and amber. And most of the umbrellas have wrist straps, too. There must be a lot of absent-minded professors riding the cars.

I asked the custodian of lost articles to tell me the strangest thing ever brought in. He wrinkled his brow and decided that the artificial leg somebody lost and never missed took the prize. A mislaid glass eye comes a close second, not to mention the several sets of false teeth which are waiting for anybody who has trouble eating his Sunday dinner.

Then I asked him to tell me the largest thing ever lost. It was a full size bicycle some boy managed to lift into a street car and then forgot to take home with him. Baby carriages have been lost on the cars too, but that is easy to explain; the babies grow up and learn to walk.

And the medical student who lost a skull (not his own) on a street car has not called for it yet.

And can you tell me just how anybody would lose

a wrist watch? Easy, the strap breaks. I saw a large drawer full of fine watches, another drawer of eyeglasses still unclaimed, a whole room full of gloves and rubbers and carpenter's tools and victrolas and hats and coats and crutches and sundry other bric-a-brac, all of it lost, but not yet found.

Only 30 per cent of the lost articles are ever claimed by their owners. The other 70 per cent are given to the conductors or passengers who find them, sixty days following their finding. Guns and pistols are turned over to the police as crime clues. Lost liquor is poured down the drain, and perishable foods are given away in a hurry, so it is no use going back after that steak.

One thing is almost never lost—flowers. That proves that where the heart is the hand holds on, tightly.

What was the most valuable thing ever lost on the Boston street cars? It was a package containing $20,000 worth of bank stock. And the messenger boy came back for it in a hurry.

Did I say that stock was the most precious thing ever lost?

I beg your pardon. While I stood there at the lost and found desk I saw something more precious, found after being lost. A little girl in a sky-blue coat and with yellow curls came in with her mother and asked, "Mister, did you find a little plaid purse? I lost it on the street car and it had a handkerchief and a quarter in it. I got it for Christmas and I lost it the first time I took it outdoors. Do you think you found it, sir?" Her face was so sad I found my hand rummaging into my trousers for another quarter, but I did not have to pull out my hand, for the lost and found man looked at a fresh pile of purses, clutched a little plaid one, and asked her, "Is this it?" I wish you could have seen that five-year-old girl's face. She could hardly speak, but she gave that little purse a fond kiss. Then her mother reminded her to say thank you, and they were off, skipping down the stairs.

"That's the fun of this job," said the lost and found man, "seeing somebody change from grave to gay, when they have found what was lost."

But in a world like this we can lose a great many things besides our rubbers or our false teeth.

For one thing we can lose our sanity. That is not hard in an insane world. And the only way I know to find one's sanity after it has been lost is to take a long view of life, to see far ahead to a day when the wrong will be set right, when good will begin to win over evil, when peace will begin to take the place of war, when moderate plenty will begin to supplant poverty and misery. Unless you believe in that ultimate hope, of course you will lose your sanity. Unless some personal and public progress is possible we all live in a madhouse, crazily careening toward annihilation. But when we discover a reason for living that is bigger than we are, when we give ourselves up to something better than we are, then we find our sanity, even after we have lost it.

In the next place it is easy to lose patience. Sometimes it is good business to lose patience. I fancy that slavery was swept off the face of America because somebody lost patience with it, among others Garrison and Lincoln. Some day war will be outmoded because some of us lose patience with it. Whenever it is something you can do something about, go right ahead and lose patience over it; that may help, that may be the goad to wake you up and put you in action. When somebody loses patience with greasy-handed corruption in business or politics or religion then something good begins to happen. Indeed, I dare say that one of our faults as citizens today is that it takes us so long to lose patience with rotten things.

But there is another sphere of life where we have no right to lose patience. That is when we cannot possibly help the situation by our loss of patience. Some of you are sick in bed, very sick. And your biggest difficulty is in being a patient patient. Active in mind and used to doing things, you can hardly put up with this business of being in bed twenty-four hours a day. Now I am up and healthy, and it is poor sport for me to give you a lot of cheap advice, but this I know, that if you have lost patience with something you cannot help you will find no peace at all until you find that patience again within the power

of great religion and great faith, and until you have
a great hope that some day soon you will be better
than you are now. There is one other reason for not
losing your patience. Your patience will make it
easier for those who so lovingly care for you. And if
you cannot really be patient, just pretend to be. Even
that will help. David Grayson has a little book called
Adventures in Solitude, which is the story of what he
did when he was in the hospital for eight months
with orders not to see visitors. At first he lost patience,
then he found it again and spent the eight months
recalling to mind his favorite verses of poetry, writing letters to famous people which he answered himself. One day he had a grand time thinking what he
would do if he had a million dollars. That helped his
patience.

Another thing some of us lose is our sense of direction. We do not know just where we are going, but
we are on our way. That happens often in the complex life of our American cities today. Filing claims
in a cabinet all day or tightening nut number 56
to bolt number 57 does not help us keep a sense of
direction. We may not be badly lost, but we are like
Daniel Boone, who was once asked if he had ever
been lost in the forest. He answered, "Never lost,
but once in a while bewildered." Most of us know
what he meant by "bewildered." For sooner or later
all of us get lost one way or another. One is lost in
doubt and does not know which way to turn, another
is lost in debt and cannot get out of debt's prison house

of fear of more debt, another is lost in sorrow with no laughter in sight anywhere, no joy under heaven and no zest on earth. Somebody else is lost in loneliness, more oppressive every day, with no one near to understand or help. It is the greatest miracle on earth when somebody who has been lost, is found. It is never easy, but thank God it is possible. Even when we are lost in sin, over our heads and drowning in our own misdoing, there is hope that we may find ourselves, or be found, before it is too late.

Here is an old story, from a very old book, about somebody who was lost, and then found.

A man had two sons. The younger said to his father, "Father, give me my share of the property." So he divided his property between them. Not many days later, the younger son gathered up all he had, and went away to a distant country, and there he squandered his property in wanton living. After he had spent it all, a severe famine arose in that country, and he began to be in want. He hired himself out, and was sent into the fields to tend pigs. And he was ready to fill himself with the pods the pigs were eating, and no one would give him anything. When he came to himself he said, "I will get up, and go to my father, and say to him, 'Father, I have sinned against heaven, and in your eyes; I no longer deserve to be called your son; treat me like one of your hired men'."

And he got up and went to his father. But while he was still a long way off, his father saw him, and pitied him, and ran and fell on his neck, and kissed him. His son said to him, "Father, I have sinned against heaven, and in your eyes; I no longer deserve to be called your son; treat me like one of your hired men." But his father said to his servant, "Make haste and get out the best robe, and put it on him, and put a ring on his hand, and shoes on his feet, and get the calf we are fattening and kill it, and let us feast and celebrate, for my son was dead, and he has come to life; he was lost, and he is found!"

That happened once. It has happened since. It can happen again. The lost can be found.

We never seem to know the meaning of something precious until we have lost it.

WILL GOD BLESS AMERICA?

I SEE a new wave of ardent patriotism sweeping our country. One sign says, "America, love it or leave it." Another declares, "If you don't like our form of government, they are still running boats to Europe." And the flag-makers report a boom in demand for the Stars and Stripes in all their glory.

This is my most vivid impression after a summer's tour of ten thousand miles on gasoline and rubber, from the Atlantic to the Pacific. "Isn't it great to be an American?" That slogan is in the store windows, car windows, on the billboards of the U. S. A.

One evening in Medford, Oregon, where they grow luscious pears, I enjoyed a night baseball game, brightly illumined with flood lights. A good negro team from Kansas City, led by Satchel Foot Paige, played a white man's team from Medford. During the seventh inning stretch we stood up and sang with full hearts, "God Bless America." Seldom have I been so deeply moved with emotion while negroes and white men stood in reverence singing a song about America written by a Jew, Irving Berlin.

At every little crossroads, in the Great Plains, on the Rocky Mountains, over the Painted Desert, Americans are singing that good song.

But who is an American? Satchel Foot Paige, that negro pitcher, he is an American. Irving Berlin, the Jew, he is an American. That Swedish farmer in Minnesota who grows good corn, he is an American. The Hopi Indians tripping a light fantastic toe through their snake dances at Grand Canyon, they were Americans, long before the rest of us. As Will Rogers used to say of his Indian blood, "My ancestors did not come over on the *Mayflower,* but they met the boat."

The Chinese girl in San Francisco's Chinatown who sold us the blue-gold embroidery, she is an American. And the Japanese farmer in Oregon, he is an American now. Who is an American? Every man child and girl child born on this fair soil, no matter who their parents were. And any man or woman of foreign birth who can pass the tests of American citizenship, these are all Americans.

As long as we can *all* stand up *together* and sing, God will bless America.

For whether God blesses America or not does not depend so much upon God as it does upon us Americans. God is ready to bless anybody, any time. He is no respecter of persons or nations. He does not play favorites. God wants to bless all of us, but by the way we live, by the mistakes we make, we often prevent God's blessing from becoming manifest.

The plain truth is that God has blessed America in about every way He can. The harvest is altogether rich and bountiful. I saw the corn in Iowa stretching high and green for miles on end. I saw the wheat in golden waves of fully matured heads in the fertile Mississippi Valley. I tasted the ripe, full flavored fruit of Oregon. I saw the grapes of Southern California and, as they ripened in the field, there was no wrath in them. God has blessed America with a wheat crop twice as large as we can use in domestic consumption and yet we human beings have so badly bungled our distribution system that somebody, yea many a body, will go hungry this winter while wheat rots in the granaries. God has done his part. When will we do our part?

Not only has God blessed America with a bountiful harvest, but He has also blessed us with the most infinite variety of scenery in the world. One day we roasted with the heat in South Dakota, the next we froze in the high passes of the Big Horn Mountains. And at Mount Rainier in Washington we played catch with snowballs. One day we drove eighteen miles without a turn to the right or left; that was in the southern desert. Another day in Northern California we twisted and turned along a coast road where a sign warned us, "Caution, sharp curves and steep grades for the next sixty-three miles." Among the giant redwoods of California I walked into the forest and looked up at the tallest known tree in the world, three hundred sixty-four feet. In the Badlands nothing can grow except cactus and sagebrush, but in Southern California the gardens are exotic in color and profusion.

What is the garden spot of America? I think it is Yellowstone Park with its bears begging for food on the roadway, its sapphire pools shimmering in the sunlight, its hundred and one geysers spraying in soft cascades against the blue sky, its canyon deep cut in the earth to leave red and yellow stonework sparkling in the morning. Yellowstone is as near to heaven as I expect to get on earth. I shall never forget Old Faithful shooting skyward one hundred and sixty feet, white loveliness against the setting sun. Thank God for America. You and I are very lucky to be here.

The wild flowers of the Yellowstone are a joy in themselves. A ranger showed us the Achilles flower, then told us about the school boy who wrote an essay on Achilles. He meant to say, "Achilles' mother dipped him in the River Styx and he came out invulnerable." But the boy got things mixed a little and wrote, "Achilles' mother dipped him in the River Stynx and he came out intolerable."

This is the America we love, infinite variety. Variety of racial strains among our people. Variety of geography from the Atlantic to the Pacific. Variety of cultural interests. Variety of occupations from the banker at his glass-topped desk in New York to the cowboy on his bucking broncho in Wyoming. I stand in awe of the western cowboy who is at home on the range and likes it. At a rodeo in Custer I saw a cowboy stand on his head and throw his lariat over the head of a horse running past at a full gallop. The

strangest occupation I heard of was a man in Oklahoma who made his living betting on his fighting
cocks. Attaching small hooks to the spurs of a cock,
he placed it in the cockpit to fight the enemy rooster.
The winner collected the bet. Not what one would
call a parlor pastime. In the Southwest, Indian wom-
en stand beside the road holding up small pieces of
pottery, hoping the motorist will stop, back up, and
buy. But most of us drive so fast we are out of sight
of the Indian squaw before we can stop the car. At
Bonneville Dam on the Columbia River I watched a
man make his living counting salmon as they swam up
the Columbia to spawn. He sits in a little box atop the
dam, at the crest of the fish ladders, low steps with
water flowing over them, counting the salmon as they
jump up the ladders into the upper river. How many
kinds of work it takes to make America! Infinite variety. And that variety ought to be our country's salvation. We shall not lean too heavily on one industry, on
one farm product. So our variety of racial strains is our
hope. We shall not glorify one race, white or black or
red, over any other race.

Will God bless America? Only if we Americans
work out our own salvation by productive agricul-
ture, manufacture and a wise culture that puts the
prime emphasis upon the worth of human personality.

In other words the old-fashioned road of hard
work is the way to bless America. No easy-going pan-
acea will make us a blessed nation. Somewhere in

the west I saw this sign on the roadside, "God bless America with the Townsend Plan." How characteristic that is. We want God to bless America our own private way. We concoct our little plan for making ourselves comfortable, then try to push over the idea upon the nation.

In the last place it seems fair that we ought not to ask God to bless America only. That would be like praying, "God bless me," without much caring what happened to anybody else. God bless America, yes, but why can we not pray also, God bless England, mother of our speech, land of our Pilgrim fathers, so beset by trouble in this dark hour? And God bless France, fair among the nations and our sister of many sorrows. We remember her past glories and pray for her spiritual renewal. And God bless Italy, rich in her gifts of beauty and art. Direct her rulers into wisdom and righteousness. God bless Russia, coming out of bondage through days of storm. Guide her out of passion, prejudice and plunder into reverence and truth. And God bless Germany, now so misguided and far from the path of peace and humility. We remember her past glories of music and art and science and we fervently pray that the dominion over her of falsehood and prejudice and of the sword may be speedily broken.

God bless China that her hurts may be healed, her starving people may be fed. God bless Japan that she may not be self-destroyed by blood violence.

So we do not stand alone. We ask no blessings for

ourselves that we do not wish for all men everywhere. We are not a tribe in a valley, we are brothers on a planet, living close to each other by the power of the airplane and the radio. In more senses than were ever true before in the history of the world, we live or die together.

Will God bless America? You and I will answer from our windows on Every Street.

THE TEMPERAMENT IN SAN JUAN

The temperament in San Juan has never been above 94 degrees nor below 62 degrees in U. S. weather bureau history.

Misprint in the *Back Bay Leader*.

THAT is decidely the kind of temperament to have, in San Juan or in Tompkins Corner or in Anytown. A temperament that never rises above 94 nor falls below 62.

I hope the type-upsetter made that mistake on purpose for it is too good a mistake to be an accident.

The nice thing about a temperament like that is it never rises to the boiling point, 212 degrees. It gets just nicely warm, 94, but it never gets hotheaded. It never boils over, temperamentally speaking. How much we all need that kind of temperament, capable of real enthusiasm up to 94 but never flying off into a tantrum of boiling rage at 212.

Much of the trouble in this world is caused by hotheadedness, somebody's temperament rising up to 212 and causing a tempest in a teapot. The World War started because somebody got hot-headed at

Serajevo on June 28, 1914, and pulled a trigger that set off the powder keg. And if there is no world war again it will be because enough leaders and followers keep their temperaments down near 94 degrees, instead of up around 212. Who can calculate the things people do and say when they are in a rage, to atone for which they would later cut off their right hands? How many homes are split wide open because somebody gets hot-headed at breakfast and starts for Reno before waiting to cool off?

Calling upon Abraham Lincoln in his study one day, a friend furtively reported, "Mr. Lincoln, Stanton says you are a fool." Instead of flying into a rage, Lincoln answered quietly, "If Mr. Stanton says so, it must be true." Lincoln's temperament never rose above 94.

The pity is that often very little things will send supposedly very big men into a handsome rage over almost nothing. Clarence Day reports that when his father used the telephone, "He usually got angry at Central. He said she was deaf, she was stupid. If she said a number was busy, he'd protest, 'Busy? I'm busy too. I can't sit here waiting all day.' "

In a little book of Cardinal O'Connell's, *Vigor in Arduis,* he says clearly what I am trying to say now, "You must keep your heads clear, your minds alert, but above all, keep cool during these trying times." Cool heads would spare many a broken heart.

Hot-headed anger not only abridges a man's power to think straight, it spoils his digestion and sours his disposition. And to try to help any cause by getting mad about it is like pouring oil on fire.

And rage is usually blind, too. In Paris during the war a mob of super-patriots tore a restaurant to pieces because someone said he had found a jar of biscuits with a label marked, "Hindenburg Biscuits," on the restaurant table. After all the uproar someone looked at the label more closely and discovered that what it really said was, "Edinburgh Biscuits." That was different, but it did not rebuild the restaurant.

The second good thing about the temperament in San Juan is that it never falls below 62. It never gets down to freezing, 32. You will not die of chilblains or cold feet.

And an icy temperament gets us into just about as much unhappiness as hot-headedness. It is of a different variety. It leaves us lonely and unloved, to die of dignity. Nothing takes the fun out of life more than an iceberg of a person who chills the air for miles around his awesome presence and dampens every enthusiasm he meets, in himself or in somebody else. God save us from our frosted friends!

Some years ago a very famous, if a bit chilly, organist was giving a recital on a new organ. The wind was pumped by a small boy behind a screen. (There is now a national Society of Former Organ Pumpers.) At this recital the boy pumped his heart out and was glad for the intermission half-way through the program. Out in the vestry of the church the boy looked up at the great organist and ventured, "Aren't we wonderful?" The Iceberg answered, "Who's we?"

With listless steps the lad returned to his pump for the climax of the recital. The organist pressed the keys for the opening chord. Only silence came from the majestic pipes. The signal must have failed. The organist repeated it, flourished his hands upwards, then pressed again for the thunder to come. No thunder came, only a still small voice from behind the screen, yet loud enough for the whole assembly to hear, "Now who's we?" That is the fair penalty for a temperament below 62.

Now somewhere between 94 and 62 degrees there is a warm, reasoning, understanding, forgiving range of temperament which is easy to live with and which keeps this often over-heated or over-chilled world at a livable climate. It is a temperament full of the milk of human kindness and it makes home worth living in, it makes work worth doing and it makes our leisure hours resonant with laughter.

For temperament, therefore, I like San Juan.

Mark Twain described New England weather most aptly in 1876 when he spoke before the New England Society and said, "There is a sumptuous variety about the New England weather that compels the stranger's admiration—and regret. The weather is always doing something here; always attending strictly to business; always getting up new designs and trying them on people to see how they will go. I have counted one hundred and thirty-six different kinds of weather inside of twenty-four hours." Then Mark

Twain described a typical weather forecast for Boston, "Probable Nor'east to Sou'west winds, varying to south'ard and west'ard and east'ard and points between; high and low barometer, sweeping round from place to place; probable areas of rain, snow, hail and drought, succeeded or preceded by earthquakes with thunder and lightning." That's New England.

Who can do justice to October in and around Boston? "October's bright blue weather" is only a piece of poetry, until you spend October in New England and live out under the deep blue skies flecked with white running clouds, watch the mellow slanting sunlight on the yellow and red of a thousand autumn hillsides, see the frost upon the pumpkin, feel the tang in the crisp air and taste the sparkle in the cider. That's October in New England. You open your windows and let the fragile leaves blow in to garnish your rug. You stand at your doorstep and let the fresh wind of heaven blow through your soul and make you glad to be alive in a place like this on a day like this in a time like this.

But not all is fanciful prettiness even in October, for somebody has a premonition of colder days soon coming. Out on the cinder piles of Allston stoop-shouldered old women and sober-faced children who should be doing lighter things are picking over the cinders to find a few stray lumps of coal for winter's fires. A day's work yields grudgingly a burlap sack full of black diamonds. Then the work is not over;

the sack must be lugged home in the early twilight. October is not all "bright blue."

And fair weather in October takes another toll in forest fires when the woods are dry and ready for any careless match or spark. No man would ever be careless again if he could view only once the charred hillside with black, ghostly-shaped timbers; the only vestige of what was once the fair green wood. Five years after a bad fire the undergrowth has started and the carpet is green, but the dead monsters, stark naked, still overtop the green and make perpetual reminder of "what a great matter a little fire kindleth."

So, hail to a temperature like New England's, with plenty of steam in the summer and ice in the winter and sunshine in October.

And hail to a temperament like San Juan's, never above 94 nor below 62.

LIKE A RIVER

A RIVER is something more than a stream of water flowing downhill to the sea; it is a highway for the ships and the dreams of mankind. It is a trysting place for lovers and a means of exchange of commodities and cultures. The history of almost any community is the history of the rivers that flow past it to the sea. And for each of us, our personal history is often wrapped around some familiar stream that bore us far away on joyous adventures of body and mind.

Three rivers are especially dear to me: the Charles, the Niagara and the Colorado.

The Charles reminds me of the seven ages of the individual man. Born in a hillside spring some thirty miles southwest of Boston, the Charles, like a man named Charles, begins its life gurgling and laughing. Then the river, in its childhood, winds and twists playfully among the plains of Dedham and Wellesley and Newton and Watertown, quite like a child meandering in the fields and woods. Then, entering Cambridge, the river gains depth and breadth, and like a growing man, it straightens out its course and is capable of carrying responsibilities—ships and rowing shells. Sometimes the river is pressed between steep banks and rushes through in swifter turmoil. Human beings know this kind of crisis too, with the boundaries of life squeezing in. Then, near the end of its journey, the Charles widens out and moves more quietly, takes time for reflections of sun and moon and stars. At long last the river returns to the Mother who gave it birth, the Atlantic Ocean, and though the river dies, it lives on reunited with the eternal sea. So do we all move out into the eternal sea, the Life which gave us birth. Like a river, so are we.

The bridges spanning the Charles are romance in themselves. The Longfellow Bridge, where the poet "stood at midnight," is now a vast arch of steel and granite with four towers gracefully pointing skyward in the sunset. The Cottage Farm Bridge is the scene of four levels of traffic: boats on the river beneath, trains on the railroad span, cars above the trains and the evening plane to New York flying above the other three.

The Harvard Bridge is long and flat, built on a series of piers. Once it was a floating bridge built on pontoons. Now it bears an endless flow of traffic between Boston and Cambridge. Where are all the cars going? Where have they come from? And even today not everybody has a car, for any hour of day or night patient pedestrians cross that long bridge to work and play, in sun and sleet.

And all too often somebody makes the Harvard

Bridge the Bridge of Sighs, straddles the railing and jumps overboard to try to make an end of sorrow or sin. We watched the police boat grappling for a body which had at last broken free from its wretched soul. A child asked me why the woman had jumped in. I ventured, "Maybe she had no work and nothing to eat. Or maybe she had no friends and was lonesome."

"Well," added the child in his wisdom, "she won't find any friends in the river."

But what about something a little more cheerful on the river? Certainly. Sailboats. If anything ever was created by man to bring other men back to peace and sanity and contentment it is a white sailboat leaning in the wind on the Charles. And when a fleet of sailboats stretches across the river, you have a picture to heal sore eyes or broken hearts. And to get your hand on a tiller, or to feel the healthy pull of the main sheet in a good sou'wester, is to become a part of the wild winds of nature; it is to believe yourself a hand-maiden of the gods instead of nurse to a gasoline buggy.

If you are on the edge of a nervous breakdown, beg, borrow or steal a sailboat and get a good seaman to show you how to tack, luff or come about. You may get wet, but you will get back your balance and your sense of proportion.

From my window on Beacon Street I usually see nothing but pleasure boats flirting in the breeze, going nowhere in particular, but having a lot of fun doing it. The Charles is for pleasure boats.

The Niagara, on the other hand, is for burden vessels. Heavy cargo boats, loaded to the gunwales with coal or iron or lumber, pick their leaden-footed way up the narrow channels of the Niagara to the smoke-belching factories along the shore from Buffalo to Tonawanda and Niagara Falls. No white sails and fancy varnish for these burden vessels, no going any old place any old time. They have to stick to the channel for, heavy laden, they go down deep. Burden vessels are not so pretty; smoke-covered, they earn their own board because they carry more than their own weight. They carry the burdens of the world upon their crossbeams and keels. They keep us fed and warm and sheltered, and if we have to make a choice, we had better vote to keep the cargo carriers afloat and put the pleasure boats in the shed.

But we do not have to make it either or. There is room on the river for both the pleasure boat and burden vessel. There is room in any life, I hope, for a little sailing and a lot of hauling.

But just now, while we are thinking about it, let us take off our hats to the people we know who carry far more than their own weight in this world. They are the burden vessels; the men with the hoes and the wrenches and the scalpels in their hands, the crosscut saw and the pen. And the women carrying the family wash and the dishes, they cannot sport about in the breeze. They have to keep to the channel, and on schedule, because they are heavy-laden; they have to make port because someone is waiting for what they carry. They might like to explore the adventuresome solitary isles and the wooded shores; they might like to take their fun, but confound it, that burden, that load of responsibility is always on deck, pressing. The children are always needing something, the house is never fully straightened, the job is never done. These are the burden carriers of earth and because of what they do they make it possible for some of the rest to be pleasure boats.

One day Napoleon with his soldiers met a peasant carrying a bundle of faggots. Napoleon saw his men forcing the woman off the road by their arrogant insistence on the right of way. He reprimanded them, commanding them to step aside with the curt, "Respect the burden." He might have stooped to lift that bundle of faggots. But failing that, the next best thing is to respect the burden, whenever we see anyone carrying it.

The Grand Canyon of the Colorado is "full to the brim with hush," except when you stand deep down in the canyon beside the raging torrent of the river as it hurries on its way of yellow peril to Boulder Dam. J. B. Priestley says we Americans are foolish to go to Switzerland when we have the Grand Canyon within such easy reach. He thinks it the scenic wonder of the world.

In the *Saturday Evening Post* for February 26, 1938, is the most exciting story on record about the Colorado River. It is the true story of Buzz Hol-

strom's trip down the Colorado alone, in 1937.[1]
This stream is eleven hundred miles long with three
hundred and sixty-five major rapids and countless
smaller ones. It is the world's most dangerous river.
In many of the canyons the granite sides rise sheer
from the water and the wreck of a boat would mean
no possible way of escape. It took Holstrom fifty-two
days to make the run from Green River to Boulder
Dam. The way he did it is the way you and I will
run the River of Life with its rapids and gorges, if
we are to get through.

First, he built his own boat, out of fine cedar,
light and strong. He chose his own log in the cedar
forest of Oregon, dragged it out to a sawmill and
had it cut to his own specifications. He studied designs of previous boats, then made a new design out
of experience and his own ideas. It took him six
months to build that boat, fifteen feet long and five
feet wide, with a small cockpit but mostly decked
over. It was flat-bottomed and weighed four hundred
and fifty pounds. He knew just how much strain
every joint and rib and seam would stand.

So in the River of Life, each one must build his
own boat. We cannot borrow a boat from somebody
else. We must study the designs of other people's
philosophies of life, see where they failed or succeeded, study the verdicts of history, then build our
own boat out of our tears and laughter, out of our
own success and failure, out of our own joy and sor-

[1] Printed by permission of the *Saturday Evening Post*.

row. No two people in the world are alike in face or
experience or in soul or mind, therefore no two
people will have exactly the same philosophy of life.
Often people come to their minister, asking him to
give them a faith to live by, a simple, adequate philosophy of life. No minister can do that. He can give
advice and tell what his own philosophy is; he can
give them a meal or a job, but a framework of conviction to live by is personal business. Each one must
build it for himself.

Second, Holstrom practised on the rough water
near his home, the Salmon and the Rogue Rivers.
Thus he was ready for rougher water on the Colorado.

So in the River of Life, the only way to meet a
big crisis is to practise by meeting little crises as they
come along. Waiting for a big chance is utter foolishness because there are numberless little chances all
about us, chances for showing our courage and skill
and patience and understanding.

Third, when Holstrom ran the rapids, sometimes
he drifted with the current and sometimes he cut
across it, to avoid hidden rocks and treacherous
whirlpools.

So in the River of Life. Good judgment in knowing when to go with public opinion and when to
cut across it is the most needed kind of judgment for
any man. It may cost a great deal to cut against public opinion. It did for Jesus and Galileo and Coper-
nicus. And in the River of Life a man may lose his

body by cutting across public opinion, but he may save his soul.

Fourth, Holstrom threw overboard the excess baggage, the impedimenta, things he could get along better without; the heavy tent was unnecessary because he could sleep in only the sleeping bag. Out went a heavy iron pulley, extra cakes of soap, a side of bacon, three cans of chili, three cans of corned beef. These were things he decided he could do without.

So in the River of Life, the most important piece of furniture is the waste basket, knowing what to throw away and put out of one's attention. For want of this ability to be done with some unnecessary things thousands of lives are frittered away in trivial matters, never getting down to the main business of living. To know which magazines to buy and which ones are better not bought, to know when to turn the radio off, and what to turn to when it is on, these are the kind of things not taught in many schools, except the school of observed experience and good common sense.

Fifth, Holstrom knew enough to draw aside from the river to rest and relax and gain perspective and power for the next day's rapids. He did not try to run the river in one day. As he rested one evening beside the Colorado, looking up at the clear stars above the desert, he commented, "The peace and friendliness and physical relaxation wiped out the hardship of the day."

So in the River of Life, we die for want of a place

of retreat, a place where we can get out of the rapids
for reflection and a view of something above the
river—stars and sky and past and future and the
world of dreams to be found in memory and meditation. Without this place of soul rest the spirit dies
of strangulation or overwork, the life burns out for
want of renewal.

These are the ways Holstrom got through the river
of the Colorado alone.

And these are the ways we shall get through the
River of Life alone.

PICKING UP THE PIECES

THE morning after the wild storm found all of us engaged in the same occupation. Bank president, housewife and messenger boy, we were all levelled to one vocation—picking up the pieces.

Some picked up big pieces, like the riggers who wielded torches to cut loose a mammoth electric sign which had crashed across the street opposite Symphony Hall.

Some picked up little pieces, the flotsam and jetsam of tin roofs and stray bricks and odd lamp posts which a million home dwellers found on their front lawns, or draped ungracefully across their back fences.

Weather vanes grew tired of pointing the way the hurricane was blowing, broken slate spiraled in the whirling eddies and a stone fell from the tower of the church, sinking itself a foot into soft earth, instead of into someone's skull. We have been picking up these pieces.

Out on the Charles River disconsolate yachtsmen are picking up the pieces, looking for the rudder or cushions from the once good ship, *Sweet Adeline,* or *Dulciana,* or *Idle Hour.* It will take more than all the king's horses and all the king's men to put *Dulciana* together again.

You can watch Mr. Goodly-girth next door reducing his belt line by wrestling with the fallen timber on his back lot. He will be a handsomer man for having bandied a buck saw on live oak!

Another blessing of a hurricane is its reminder of how greatly we take electric lights for granted. While busy linemen picked up the pieces of wire and cable many a family enjoyed the temporary, romantic inconvenience of candlelight. Let them enjoy it while they may, before the glaring bulb comes alive again. Conversation flows easily to the rhythm of the wavering candle flame, hearts beat a little faster and perhaps a little warmer, fond faces take on a new charm in the soft, changing shadows.

But do not let the romanticism of the candlelight run away with you:

> "Yes," I answered you last night;
> "No," this morning, sir, I say:
> Colors seen by candlelight
> Will not look the same by day.

Picking up the pieces!

Here is a true story about the fine art of picking up the pieces.

Once upon a long time ago, in a modest house in the Riverside section of Buffalo a six-year-old boy was playing horse and driver with his jolly father one indoor evening.

The boy was the horse. A stout string under his shoulders was the harness. Father was the driver, holding the ends of the string for reins.

Mother, fortunately or unfortunately, depending on your point of view regarding this race, was upstairs in the sewing room.

The race course circuit was free and open. Through the hall into the kitchen, then past the swinging door into the pantry and on into the dining room. With gathering speed the parlor came next, the draperies into the hall were a mile-post, as it were, and then on around, again and again, with the horse almost a runaway and the driver in merely nominal control of his steed. Six full laps around the circuit were without incident, except to loosen the foundations of the house.

But on the seventh lap, the horse smelled the oats in the stable, so to speak, put a little extra careless speed into the curve from the parlor into the hall, swung a little too wide and tripped over the table on which stood the ancient family lamp, in all its decorative, polychrome splendor.

What a lamp that was! Ornate brass base, then a massive globe of crimson glass etched with flowers. Above the globe a girdle of lacy brass work and, crowning the top, a pear-shaped globe in jade green, over-topped by a silken shade bordered with gold fringe. This Victorian monster reached halfway to the ceiling, until the runaway horse tipped the table that fateful night.

At first it swayed, then it arched to the floor in a dizzy curve and crashed into a hundred pieces of broken colored glass.

The horse and driver stood dumb, sober at last, if a little late. Heavy footsteps started down from the sewing room. Criss-cross looks said what words did not need to say. A tear or two moistened someone's cheek. Resolutions about no more horse-racing in the house.

Then, together, they began picking up the pieces.

And with the picked-up pieces that lamp was destined for a reincarnation. Creative imagination did it. Taking three ordinary earthen jars, the lady-from-the-sewing-room covered the outside of each jar with a layer of plastic putty. She then set the broken pieces of glass into the soft putty, with considerable care for design and color harmony. Now those three vases do perpetual service as flower containers and are witness to what can happen when somebody picks up the pieces and mixes with them imagination.

Truth to tell, the jars are more useful than the decorative monstrosity of a lamp, in its senility, ever could have been.

Be sure of this, whether by hurricane, or somebody's careless play, or by sheer hard luck, some day your pretty lamp, your dream tower, your picture of perfect comfort may be tipped over and shattered into a thousand pieces around your feet.

What will you do when that happens?

Will you go to pieces yourself?

Or will you pick up the pieces and put them together again with patience and imagination, making the earthen jar, useful perhaps beyond your dreaming, take the place of the dream lamp?

Man, when that little business you had put your money and your head and your heart into, broke under your feet in the depression, what did you do? Did you go to pieces, have a nervous breakdown and lean on somebody's shoulder? Or did you pick up the pieces and start again on a shoestring?

Woman, when the little home you lived in and loved and worked for is shattered by hard-luck tragedy and you moan, "Why should this happen to me?" do you go to pieces or do you pick up the pieces?

Son, when you have made a bad mistake, when you have tripped over your own worst weakness and made a fool of yourself, what will you do about it? Will you go to pieces, from bad to worse? Or will you pick up the pieces of your broken reputation and start over again with a new and better design for living? Better by sad experience.

Daughter, when a hurricane of disillusion hits you and someone you trusted proves he cannot be trusted, what do you do about it? Do you go to pieces or do you pick up the pieces of whatever faith you can grasp, faith in yourself, faith in a Power above your own, faith in the way of the Cross to lead you on to new truth, faith in the ultimate rightness of things?

After a hurricane on Beacon Street, or after a hurricane in your own inner soul, there is nothing else so worthwhile doing, as to pick up the pieces.

MY GRANDFATHER'S HOUSE

THEY are moving a house across Commonwealth Avenue. And it seems to take more trouble than building a new house on the new site might cost. Trolley cars are halted for half the night to let the wires be taken down to get the house across. Traffic is detoured for twenty-four hours for the same purpose. A dozen men work all day and night to get the house over the crossing.

Which reminds me of my grandfather's house—and a rude surprise.

The summers of my childhood were spent in and around his old house in the rich farming country of Ontario, in a little village called Delhi. Weather-beaten, dark gray picket fences marked the corner. A path wound in through the tall grass to the door sill, worn down two inches by the feet of three generations. The unpainted clapboards were almost black. Green moss clung to the corners of the roof with its curled, black shingles. Two huge elms shaded the house from the summer sun. Inside, wide floor boards creaked at every step and bumps rose in the boards where old-fashioned nails kept the wood from wearing down just around them. Narrow, precipitous stairs led up to the low-ceilinged dormer bedrooms with their huge feather beds. Patchwork quilts were hardly necessary on summer nights, but they were part of the ancient scene. The kitchen usually smelled of dried apples or smoked ham.

One summer, during my college years, I had a sudden nostalgia for the house I had missed for so many years, so I drove across the Peace Bridge at Buffalo toward my grandfather's house.

Soon the country school hove in sight, then the canning factory, next the old Anglican Church with its soft red brick and its colored windows, and upon the instant I had come to the corner with the big elm trees. But instead of shading my grandfather's house, they looked down upon an empty pit which had once been the fruit cellar, now overgrown with weeds and brush.

My heart sank into the pit with the weeds. Had the house burned without my hearing of it? I hurried across to the neighbor's. She explained, "Mortimer Heath's house was moved several years ago, over to King Street."

"Where is King Street?" was all I wanted to know. I found it on the other side of town, but it looked to me like a street of entirely new houses. I could see no trace of my grandfather's weather-beaten homestead.

At the first modern bungalow I asked, "Do you know if Mortimer Heath's house was moved to this street?"

"Certainly, sir," she said. "That's it across the street, with the rainbow colored roof."

I looked, and my heart fell deeper into the pit than ever. I looked at a house of pink stucco, with the roof in that frightful zigzag rainbow-hued tar paper that strains one's eyes. A cement block foundation looked as new as today's newspaper, and a porch adorned the front, approached by a hard concrete walk instead of a cool earthen path. And there were no elm trees to shade this new monstrosity from the sun.

With heavy step I rang the new doorbell and asked the prim young mother whose husband had bought my grandfather's house, if it was really true. She ushered me in on the strength of my story and the first thing she showed me was the ceiling of the living room where, she explained, "We have let the old oaken beams show through."

I felt much better after that. And I have felt continually better since.

The outside of the house had changed with the changing fashions of architecture, but the interior oaken beams that held that new house together were the same beams my grandfather had hewn out of the forest.

So the outer circumstances of life alter with time, but the same interior qualities of character hold life together today that once held life together when your grandfather was a boy and when Noah was a man.

Progress means change if you are talking about

clothes or cars or book covers. But progress also means constancy.

What are the inner beams that held life together then and will hold life together now? And without which any house of life, new or old, will crumble into dust?

The first is personal integrity. Nothing can take its place. Manners will help but manners do not make the inner man dependable. There are charming sinners who on the outside get by, but who in the interior places of their minds and souls are rotten and worm eaten. Personal integrity is as old-fashioned as the pyramids, and as up-to-date as television. It is the center beam of the house of life.

The second beam is friendship. Friendship for all kinds of people, good and bad, black and white, rich and poor. There is no other way we can live together on earth except by increasing friendship and decreasing enmity. Without friendship between persons and classes and nations we shall be lost in a welter of blood and iron.

The third beam is the Bible. No new book will put it out of style. As long as the Bible with its Ten Commandments, its Psalms and its New Testament is the best seller in the world there is some hope of our ultimate salvation. The Epicurean materialism of the twentieth century is trying to outmode the Bible, but it will not be put by.

Felix Riesenberg was once apprenticed on the training ship *St. Mary* anchored at Hellgate near

New York. As ship librarian he had special privileges of residence in the cabin where the books were kept. Shortly before Christmas a box of jams and cakes and fruit came to Felix from his mother and he wondered where he could store the treasure so that no shipmates would hi-jack the precious stuff. Opening a seldom used cabinet in the library he found fifty dusty Bibles marked on the first white page, "Gift to the training ship, *St. Mary,* from the Bible Society." The Bibles looked as though they had not been opened since the day they were thus stamped. Felix knew they would not be missed.

So, looking about to be sure he was alone, he opened the nearest porthole, reached for the first Bible and dropped it out into the tide. Twenty, thirty, forty, forty-nine, and then fifty Bibles dropped through the porthole. Felix dusted his hands and then stowed away his gastronomic treasure in the space where the Bibles had been. Just as he closed the cabinet doors and smiled at his own creative resourcefulness, a deep voice boomed down the hatchway, "What's going on down there?"

Felix called out innocently, "Nothing, Captain. Why?"

"Come up on deck and see why!"

Felix hurried up, peered overside, and saw to his horror, moving off with the tide through Hellgate, a flotilla of the Gospel, fifty Bibles nicely spaced about ten yards apart, arching in a beautiful, slowly moving curve.

All Felix could say to the glowering captain was, "I'm sorry, Captain, I thought they would sink."

The Word will not sink, even in a day like this, for it is the third beam which will hold life together.

My grandfather's house has not died. It has gone through a reincarnation.

TAKING A CHANCE

FROM my window I see people taking chances. I see a rash motorist taking a chance on getting through the yellow light just before it turns red. He will get by, unless the officer is standing in the shadow by the drug store. Then I hear that familiar, chilling whistle and another fool has been caught taking chances.

Sometimes fools on foot take chances crossing the heavy lines of traffic and I say they take their lives in their hands. Sometimes they get by with it. Once in a while they get hit.

Some take a chance with their health, eating anything and drinking anything that gives a taste thrill whether it makes a clean, strong body or not. No man can say, "I'll eat what I like and make my body take it." He has to deal with the laws of bio-chemistry and nutrition. Our hospitals are full and our doctors' offices crowded with people, some of whom are paying a high price for taking chances with their health. Sleep to them is a waste of time, outdoor exercise is a bore, meant for children and fresh air fans. What a chance they take, for getting sick!

Millions of fools take chances with their money. We call that gambling. Sometimes we call it speculative stock investment; sometimes it is betting on games or horses or dogs; sometimes it is paying money for policy tickets; sometimes it is cards for money; sometimes it is the shell-game—by any name it is just as sour. It is gambling whenever we play our stakes and expect to win a money profit without doing anything to earn that profit in productive goods or skills.

And if you will accept my humble judgment, one big reason why we are all of us in such an economic chaos and financial hocus pocus is because so many of us are gambling with our money, one way or another.

And often it is other people's money with which we gamble. Every gambler gets driven to borrowing sooner or later, then he loses what he borrowed. Or a husband gambles money which in all fairness belongs to his wife and children. Every clergyman in New England could show you a family brought to the brink of ruin by some father whose money has gone to the dogs or to the horses or into the jackpot, or for the winning number which did not win. And the thousand losers in the sweepstakes never get their pictures in the papers. Just the *one* winner.

The trouble is that this taking a chance is a disease which gets into the blood like measles or malaria, and a man who begins by betting a quarter ends up by betting the shirt off his back and gambling his last dollar from the savings bank. It is almost impossible to keep moderate about it.

This gambling mania is no local epidemic, either, so much the worse. It seems to be almost world wide, among those who are susceptible to the germ. In England the tendency is more virulent than in America, where lottery tickets and betting on races are common stuff, even among people who do not know the difference between a chestnut horse and a horse chestnut.

And I am informed that at Monte Carlo they have been obliged to abolish the hymn boards in the Church of England because the numbers were too tempting to the gamblers who were taking church on their way to the roulette wheels.

Everywhere, every day, somebody is taking chances with somebody's money, and like as not somebody else gets hurt.

I think I see why the gambling fever gets such a hold on poor mortals. It is because there is so little pioneer excitement in modern life, so little call for the taking of natural chances the way Daniel Boone did, or Kit Carson or our covered wagon ancestors. Much of the physical danger and adventure has oozed out of life, replaced by "Safety First," and doorbells and superheated airliners and canned goods on the shelf. Nobody has to go out and scare up a partridge before we can have lunch. All we need is a can opener. Now it is because we have perforce so eradicated this sense of thrilling, outward adventure that gambling satisfies the urge to take a chance.

Our grandparents found adventure in the primeval forest. Our grandchildren will find adventure in the funny papers. At a great conference of young people I once asked them to tell me what they thought of when I spoke the word, "Adventure." "Lindbergh" was the first answer, "Admiral Byrd" was the second; then a high voice far back shouted, "Popeye the sailor."

In a world like this, where natural physical adventure is so rare, what kind of chances can we take? Where can we find adventure to make our blood tingle and our minds crackle with the thrill of living? Here are my simple suggestions.

First there is the adventure of a game, outdoor or indoor, mental or physical. Until you know the sheer fun of playing a hard game just for the fun of it, you have missed the first adventure available to you.

Then there is the adventure of the mind, of reading good books, of thinking out new answers to old questions—that can be as exciting as cutting a trail through the wilderness. Adventure is not in the wandering foot, or flying fist only, adventure is also in the aching heart and the questing mind. The adventures of a hobby will give you an undreamed-of thrill.

The adventure of religion will open a new world of spiritual beauty to anyone who is willing to pay the price, to take the chance.

The adventure of friendship is worth trying, for

loneliness is the bitterest draught the gods can pour for any poor mortal. And having even one friend makes up for almost any other loss.

But here I have come this far and I have not said much about the people who take a chance with their immortal souls, take a chance on getting away with sins they know are damning their own personalities to eternal ruin. Somehow we think we may take a chance. We ought to know better, for sooner or later our sins find us out; they come out somewhere, in our own tormented conscience, or in the ruin of those we love, or in the loss of reputation and honor and integrity. We never really get away with anything. Each good or evil in the world of spirit is marked with a price and we pay that price in full, somehow.

But there is a chance I would like all of us to take today. Take a chance on yourself, your own ability to make good in what you have started, your own power to be good, not evil, and I do not mean goody-goody. I mean clean-hearted, plain-dealing, sweet tongued and honest backboned. Take a chance on being worth knowing, and liking, and loving, and working with and living with.

Take a chance on yourself, and win! You cannot lose.

MAKE A GAME OUT OF IT

EVEN yet it is a grand old world when a horsehide-covered spheroid can push war news out of the black headlines and put the double play and the home run first in the hearts of their countrymen. It happens at least once a year in the first week of October when the world's series is played somewhere between the Mississippi and Long Island.

Instead of the daily crisis the newsboy shouts about the daily batting order. How you feel about it I do not know, but I am just enough of a small boy to give three cheers when the Big Series gets more attention than the Big War.

I think our nerves need the change.

For one blessed week the national anthem is, "Take me out to the ball game," and millions of red-blooded American men and boys get out to that game by radio, with vivid imaginations putting in the green outfield, the pitcher's windup and the fast double play, until television comes of age.

Why should we get so excited about eighteen men tossing a ball around the greensward? I know why.

Because in a world full of high social tension we need the relaxed fun of a good game. We crave a chance to get excited without having that excitement mean war. We need a way of escape for some of the emotional energy pent up within us by monotonous living. Our stalwart ancestors, from whom we are sprung, traversed the seven seas in boats that were little more than egg shells. They chased and were chased by Indians through the forest, they built log cabins with their own horny hands, without blueprints. Always there was for them adventure over the next knoll or at town meeting the next evening.

But you and I, what are our adventures? Waiting for traffic lights to turn from amber to green, taking care of file number 72x for eight hours per day, assembling part number 21 on to part number 20 with two screws for fifty weeks a year. We have so surrounded ourselves with automatic machinery and handy gadgets that most of us miss the glory of an unexpected, unpredictable adventure. Now, a rousing good game lifts a man out of this goose-step world of right foot, left foot. Man is an adventure loving animal and the pity is he gets so little of what he was born for.

Baseball helps. Other games help, too, especially the games a man takes part in himself, just for the fun of it. No matter how much we enjoy watching other players take their exercise for us (and after hard mental or physical labor nothing can be more refreshing than just this spectatoritis), there is a time to play some game for oneself even though that game be a poor variety of golf or chess or badminton. A man or a woman without a little fondness for any game at all must be a dull person to live with. In East Boston I have seen excited Italians bowling on the gray cinders beside the railroad yards.

But far more important than getting time for play out of life is the knack of putting play into life, of making even the hardest kind of work partake somewhat of the joyous elation of a game. Few hard workers seem to attain this particular Nirvana but no one can calculate the flavor and music and exhilaration of a life which has begun to make play out of work.

Strangely enough we catch the full meaning of this idea when we idiomatically speak of some kinds of work as playing. We say that Heifetz "plays" his violin. Now anybody knows that what Heifetz does with his violin is the hardest kind of work, but that work is so high a form of art that it must be "played" to be done right. So Heifetz puts into his work the fire and creative imagination and whole-souled emotion which commonly go into our playing of games. And by putting these life-saving qualities into his work he makes that work play. He plays his work.

Why should a carpenter not "play" his saw and plane with creative skill? He does when he is something more than a commonplace carpenter. Why should a typist not "play" her typewriter with some of the verve she might put into a game of tennis? She does when she is something more than ten fingers attached to a machine.

So Walter Hampden plays Cyrano de Bergerac. He puts into his portrayal the zest and heart of joyous activity. His whole personality is all there. He is not merely a voice, or a gesture, or a combination of makeup. He makes a game out of the serious business of acting.

About the unhappiest picture I know is to see someone working without any heart for that work, without even a trace of play. And millions work that way, some because their work is so utterly boring that Minerva herself could hardly make it interesting and some because they do not have the capacity to move from the category of work to play.

But when a mother makes a game out of raising her family (and only a mother can know how strenuous that game can be), when a gardener makes a game out of growing his flowers, when a messenger boy makes a game out of his job, something happens which makes life worth living and saves the soul from dying of boredom during working hours.

Getting a fair balance between work and play for the people who have an overdose of either is one of our major problems today. A few unlucky fools are so cushioned that hard work is a stranger to them and one wonders if they have discovered that, "If all the year were playing holidays, to sport would be as tedious as to work."

Playing overtime must be almost as abnormal as working overtime, and even in an age of outcry against unemployment there are people who work so hard they hardly know what it means to play. They are principally in domestic service or on the farms where few holidays are noticed, or in factories and armies rushed to death by the business of war. The ironic cruelty of this overbalance between work and play is satirically illustrated by the little verse[1]:

> The golf links lie so near the mill
> That almost every day
> The laboring children can look out
> And see the men at play.

There is something wrong when a few people can play all the time and a great many people have to work all the time.

Whatever game you play, play it as a game and not as a hardbitten battle. Play to win, of course, but play genially and try somehow to laugh over your own mistakes instead of throwing the bat over the fence or cursing the ears off your friendly enemy. I once watched two men playing croquet on a neatly trimmed ground with glorious foliage overhead. It was a scene of peace all about, but the croquet ground was a deadly battlefield, the air thick with nervous tension and grim determination. Not a word was spoken in the full half hour I stood by, not one word of congratulation on a good shot from the far corner cleanly through the wicket. Not once did a flicker of a smile soften the hard-bitten lines of their faces. I did not dare ask them the stakes of this des-

[1] Printed by permission of Henry Holt & Co., from "Portraits and Protests" by Sarah N. Cleghorn.

perate game but from what I saw I infer each was
playing for the right to decapitate the other with a
broad battle axe. Never let a game be taken too seriously. This light-heartedness is the watermark of an
amateur. When you get paid for playing, then you
may have to take it a little more seriously. But never
let the money get more important than the game.

H. V. Morton once came upon a rustic peasant in
a far corner of England who was carving wooden
bowls on his doorstep. Mr. Morton asked the old
man, "How much money do you make at this business?"

The wood carver looked up calmly and answered,
"I am not making money, I am making bowls."
Such a sentiment may be a little too idealistic for
this realistic age but there is something to be said
for a man who is working for the fun of it more than
for the money in it. Professor Royce used to say of
his teaching at Harvard, "I am doing for pay what
I would do, if I could afford to, for nothing."

What kind of games shall we play when work is
done? Nobody has the right to tell anyone else just
how he must play, for nothing is more a matter of
personal choice, and no choice has a wider variety
of possibilities.

But here are three simple tests which will prove
whether our play is doing us good or ill.

First, does our playing give us a headache or a
headstart the next morning? If our playing makes
us eager to be up and at a hard job, if our playing

makes us easy to eat breakfast with, it is probably a
good game.

Second, does our game hurt anyone else? If I have
to ruin someone else's happiness or health or peace
of mind to have my fun, then my fun is too costly.
As Benjamin Franklin observed to a small boy, "You
paid too much for your whistle," so with us sometimes, we pay too much for our fun.

Third, is our kind of playing in contrast with our
everyday work to give sufficient completion to the
whole personality? Indoor work obviously suggests
outdoor play. Mental work suggests physical play.
Physical work suggests playing with the mind.

> A little work, a little play
> To keep us going—and so, good-day.
>
> A little warmth, a little light
> Of love's bestowing—and so, good-night.
>
> A little fun to match the sorrow
> Of each day's growing—and so, good-morrow.

If the serious business of living is getting you
down, try making a game out of it, and maybe you
will win!

WHO WANTS TO BE A SAINT?

ABOUT the least popular product in the spiritual markets of the world today is saintliness. Almost nobody wants to be a saint. That sounds too starchy, too monastic for red-blooded human beings. Saints were all right in their day, but we would hardly know how to act if we had to live with one. I dare say that a book on "How to become a saint" would sell only half as many copies as a book on "How to become a sinner." To the average man a charming sinner would be a far more comfortable room-mate than a perfect saint.

But suppose that we could win an enthusiastic hearing and following for the essentials of saintliness. Think what it would mean to us, one by one and million by million, if we took Paul seriously when he said we are "called to be saints." Could it be possible, somehow, that saintliness might become an attractive adventure? Dare it be true that being a saint could be as full of color as a sunrise, as full of healthy danger as climbing Mount Everest, as full of reward as the uncovering of a gold mine? What if trying to be a saint could make any one of us more interesting to ourselves and others, more useful, more alive, than trying to be a sinner?

As a matter of plain history, most of the saints were healthy, brave—even daring—men and women who stepped out to slay some dragon before that dragon could breathe its killing fire on the innocent. The idea that saintliness is an illness, something like pernicious anemia, does not come from the record of the history of the saints. It comes from the ignorant fantasy of those who say that saints were ethereal, angelic, other worldly. "Saints may have been good enough for grandmother, but they are too good for me," we say cynically. On the contrary, almost any saint you can name had iron in his blood and fire in his eye and plenty of muscle in his good right arm. Saint Paul did not travel over most of the Roman Empire in a leather upholstered limousine, preaching the good news of Jesus. He walked on his own feet, he was shipwrecked and had to swim for his life, he lived on prison diet and more than once stood against a hostile mob in a public square, without flinching. Or go with Saint Francis of Assisi into the woods of Mt. Alvernia and live for days on whatever food you can find in the forest, with no cafeteria service by day or feather bed at night. Then saintliness will seem more rugged, more enviable, more heroic, than it does to Harry Barnes who wrote, "The whole concept of sainthood is entirely out of adjustment with the modern order of things."

It is strange but true that a saint is never called a saint while he is alive. He is usually called a fool, a fanatic, a radical, an upsetter of the apple cart. And the reason for this is clear. A saint lives ahead of time. He is born too soon, as it were. So while he is alive the world fights his advanced ideas. Then after he is dead, perhaps a hundred years, the world catches up with his idea, adopts it, lives by it, and finally calls the poor fellow a saint, when he is out of earshot. H. L. Wayland has put it this way, "A saint is a man of conviction who was cannonaded while he was alive and is canonized after he is dead." A saint then is one who lives ahead of time.

By that definition, even such as you and I might be saints. Suppose you see a crisis coming in your family, or in your personal life, and you try to prepare for that crisis ahead of time, that is being a little bit of a saint in your own backyard. Or perhaps you notice, with your far-sighted eyes, that the business you are in is slipping behind the times and is due for bankruptcy. Now suppose that, seeing this impending crisis, you persuade your associates to get ready ahead of time, to so revise and modernize your business that the coming crisis will find you on the side of victory, instead of defeat. That will make you a bit of a saint, because you have lived ahead of time. Or perchance some of you are in a church which is losing its touch with people and with life, your heart is broken as you see failure after failure in meeting the needs of sick souls. Speak up and say so, think out a plan in advance, go to your minister, priest or rabbi and tell him what you think and what ought to be done to save your church and the world around

it. You may get a few upraised eyebrows for your
trouble, but you will come close to being a little
saint right now, where you are. Take one straight
look at the local government around you. Is it as
clean as a hound's tooth? Is it as honest as the day
is long on June 22nd? No, you say, the foundation
of it is rotten with graft, but everybody is afraid to
speak up. Now suppose you speak the truth as you see
it. The stones will begin to fly as they did in Saint
Stephen's direction. But you will have a grand time
and you will be almost a saint, for unless a good many
people keep insisting on honest government there will
be the devil to pay in the breakdown of public and
private morality. Or look at the whole world, racing at
break neck speed with the rumble seat of each nation's
car filled with dynamite, toward a world explosion, a
war to end civilization. We are building all the play-
things of hell for the tragic game. Where is the Voice
that sees what is coming and has the skill to stop it?
That Voice, if it could speak, and if it could be heard
and heeded, would be worth at least ten million lives;
it would save billions of dollars. And it would be the
Voice of a saint who will live ahead of time to save us
from chaos. And it will take a lot of saints to save us.

G. K. Chesterton gives us another definition. He
says a saint is one who exaggerates what the world
neglects, but needs. So today, in a world which
neglects the way of kindness for the way of brutality,
let somebody exaggerate kindness and he becomes
almost a saint. In a world where profits seem para-

mount, let somebody exaggerate the worth of personality and he becomes a saint. In a world fast becoming a wet parade, let somebody exaggerate the rewards of temperance and he becomes a saint, by Chesterton's definition. As Horace Traubel puts it, "What can I do? I can talk out when others are silent. I can say *man* when others say *money*. I can stay up when others are asleep. I can keep on working when others have stopped to play. I can give life big meanings when others give life little meanings. I can say love when others say hate. I can say every man when others say one man. What can I do? I can give myself to life when other men refuse themselves to life."

Jesus came into a world which was neglecting simplicity of religion and life. He exaggerated this simple faith in God and one's neighbors. He lived ahead of time, giving the world a religion of personal character and public honor with which the world has not yet caught up. And for doing this so great a service he was crucified. He was not called a saint; he was called to be a saint. Even yet he is not Saint Jesus. So, we are called to be saints, and the better we are at being saints the less likely it is that we shall be called saints.

Once a child was asked to define a saint. Remembering some vague figures in the stained glass windows at church, the child answered, "A saint is someone who lets the light shine through." The light of God in a dark world. We are called to be saints.

PAYMENT DEFERRED

WE ARE living in the new age of Payment Deferred.

Almost anything you want to buy, from a wheel-barrow to an apartment house, can be purchased for "Nothing down and almost nothing a week," if we are to believe the advertisements we see in every paper.

We have come to the point in America where it is the exception rather than the rule to pay cash for anything. It is much easier to say, "Charge it." And then we take ten months or two years to pay the bill. What a blessing, or a curse, thou art, sweet Payment Deferred.

The only trouble with this ultra modern system of high finance is that thousands of people with low sales resistance are supposed to be paying for a lot of things they cannot afford to buy. They are like the romantic young man who makes promises to more fair maidens than he can marry, legally. He has over-reached himself and assumed obligations he cannot fulfill.

We all hate to pay the bills handed down to us by our forebears. And yet that is exactly what we have to do so far as wars are concerned. Civil War pensions and sickness benefits, and pensions resulting from the Spanish War and World War, are even now being paid out of current tax dollars. And it will be several generations before the bills piling up around this present war are paid off by the great grandchildren of today's world. War—Payment Deferred. You pay plenty down and plenty a month from now on until Doomsday.

But the sad truth is that almost any way we turn in the world of moral values we find the sign written large for all to read, "Payment Deferred." It is inescapable.

Look for a moment at the world of heartbreak we live in today. What's wrong with it? Hitler? Yes, he is very much wrong with it. Stalin? He is no angel either. But there is something more that is wrong with this world, much deeper than Hitler or Stalin. That something is that for a long time since the world has been riding a wave of easy-going prosperity and a grab bag philosophy of get all you can for yourself and let the devil take the hindmost. And when we bought that kind of world through the lush 1920's, the sale was made on these terms, Payment Deferred. Now some of the payments are catching up with us. And we are paying through the nose, with a world torn asunder with jealousy, fear, greed, desperately holding on to what we have or trying to get what somebody else has and we want.

Not only in the realm of world affairs does this principle of deferred payment hold true, but also in

our personal conduct and choices we seldom pay cash
in full at the moment of the transaction. There is
plenty of deferred payment in our individual living.

Here is a boy of eighteen who quit school this past
week to get a high-pay job in a defense project. He
thinks he is lucky, big money and easy hours and a
grand chance to make hay while the sun shines. And
all he pays for that job is the giving up of a classroom
with its Cicero and its cube roots and what were the
causes of the War of 1812. But is that the whole cost?
That's only the first cost, the deferred payments
come later. Ten years from now a good job will be
open and he will not fill it because he slipped out of
school too soon. He will not have the background
for it. Yes, maybe he will, if he gets it outside of
school in the long hours after work.

And twenty years from now this boy who left school
for an easy money job will be laid off because of
technological changes, and when he casts about for
another field of work he finds his powers unable to
adapt themselves to new vocations and necessary
skills. He is lost in a world where the general training
he should have gained might have helped him find
his place. This is just one more Payment Deferred.

Look around you right where you live, and you
will not have to look long before you see someone
paying long after the deed was done, deferred payment for a bungled love affair, deferred payment for
one dishonesty he thought he could get away with.
In a deep sense nobody ever gets away with anything,

for deep within our souls the scales are balanced and the books audited. The down payment may be trifling, but the time payments take their full toll. In the moral world there are no bargains, as Emerson reminds us in his essay on Compensation. "The dice of God are always loaded. Every secret is told, every crime is punished, every virtue rewarded, every wrong redressed, in silence and certainty. The thief steals from himself. The swindler swindles himself."

So far I have talked more about the grim side of this philosophy of Payment Deferred.

Thank God there is a cheerful side to the whole matter, too. The Book of Ecclesiastes puts it this way, "Cast thy bread upon the waters: for thou shalt find it after many days." That is deferred payment in return for kindness scattered abroad.

No good thing that you have ever done goes completely unrewarded. The first payment to you is the inner power that action gives to your own spirit, deep inside where nobody sees. Nothing can take that away from you. And the payments deferred are the returning kindnesses that will come back to you, inevitably following a lifetime of gracious kindness toward the people who live near you or far from you.

And just as you never know when an evil deed is going to bounce back and demand another extra deferred payment out of your soul, so, thank God, you never know when an insignificant kindness is going to return to you and call you blessed. Æsop put deferred payment into the fable of the lion and the mouse, you remember. The lion, sleeping in the forest, is awakened by the mouse running over his paw, and in anger the lion is about to destroy the mouse when the mouse says, "Spare me, and some day I may help you." "But how can a little mouse help a big lion?" asks the King of Beasts. Many days later the mouse hears a growling in the wilderness. The lion has been caught in the hunter's trap. And it does not take the mouse long to bite through the ropes and set the lion free. Whereupon the lion and the mouse are friends forever and a day.

But it happens not only in fables, it happens in life. Here is a little old lady, in her lavender and lace, living on less than a meagre income in the third floor back. But the other day a delivery boy brought roses and the mail man brought a check. From whom? Twenty years ago this little lady had helped a young couple, next-door neighbors, through a hard place. Now that couple live on Easy Street and had heard that times were not the same for the old lady. The payment was deferred, but not defaulted. Sometimes it is defaulted, true, but not always.

Nowhere is this principle of payment deferred more true than in what you mothers do for your children, in guiding their feet into the way they should go. Often, the better job you do when children are small, the more they rebel and call you overstrict and unreasonable. But years later, if you have wrought with skill and foresight, your children rise up to call you blessed and your reward is sure, for you see their manhood and womanhood coming into full flower because you did good cultivating. Every parent is in for a good dose of payment deferred, one way or another. If his parenthood has been lax and indifferent he is in for plenty of payments of heartbreak in the later years. If his job has been well done, his payments will be in something more precious than gold and more fragrant than spice.

But it takes a long view to figure on the payments deferred before we incur the first cost, and we Americans today are not too good at long-distance vision.

Let each of us today, right now, take a long look ahead and see what the cost will be of what we are and what we do and what we say. How much will it cost to compromise our ideals and get by on a slipshod moral standard? What will it cost ten years from now? What will it cost to put off the straightening out of our crooked characters? What will it cost to postpone our decision as to whether we stand with Christ or the devil?

And it is not the first cost, it is the upkeep and the deferred payments that make the difference between a poor bargain and a good one.

Deferred payments are always paid by somebody, some time, somewhere.

IT IS EASIER TO TEAR DOWN A HOUSE
THAN TO BUILD ONE

FROM my window I see that it is easier to tear down a house than it is to build one. When the Ajax House Wrecking Company gets on the job, things begin to break up in a hurry. Here on old Beacon Street they have made short shrift of a once handsome mansion. It was the show place of the city fifty years ago. Today it looks as if a bomb had hit it. The wreckers topple over a wall in the time it takes to snap your fingers. But building that wall took two weeks of careful bricklaying, accurate measuring, blueprint planning. The wrecker merely touches a cornice with his crowbar, and a beautifully carved stone crumbles to the earth and shatters into a dozen fragments. Yet that cornice represented a week's skill when the stone mason chiselled out the flower design and set that stone in its right place. Yea, verily, it is easier to tear down a house than it is to build one.

It takes months to build a house that can be wrecked in a day. Building a house takes a dream, then a plan, then resources of money and materials. Building a house takes men with skill, each to his own trade. Building a house means design and pa-

93

tience and downright plain hard work that understands the purpose of the building.

But wrecking a house takes almost no planning at
all. It takes no particular resources. All you need is a
little dynamite, a few crowbars, men with muscle, and
wagons to cart off the debris.

It is easier to tear down a reputation than to build
one. To build a reputation means planning and
dreaming. To build a reputation takes skill in some
trade worth doing. Building a reputation takes hard
work over the years. You have to lay a foundation of
education and morality to build a good reputation.
But it does not take long to wreck that reputation.
One piece of dirty business, one foul play toward
someone who gets hurt, one lie that shatters its way
across the truth, one attempt at low-handed graft or
damnable dishonesty and the finest reputation can be
shattered to bits, and never again pieced together
quite so perfectly.

It is easier to tear down a home than it is to build
one. Building a home takes romance, real romance
that sees love through to its happy logical sequences.
A home begins with fluttering love words but it does
not end there. It moves soon to deep, everlasting
promises. "I love you now and I shall love you, forever." That is the promise made by those who intend
to build a home that is something more than a love
nest. And a home like that takes planning, saving,
hoping, dreaming. It counts on the new resource of
a baby one day. It is a home built on a foundation of

mutual trust and loyalty. But even a home like that can be wrecked in a day, if somebody sets out to do it by hook or crook. Some of the finest homes in the world are being wrecked today by men who think the grass is greener and the women more glamorous, whatever that means, in somebody else's yard. Other homes are being wrecked today by wives who will not stay at home long enough to give that home the attention it needs to hold it together. Some homes are being wrecked by a demon called heavy drinking. Other homes are being wrecked by gambling that gets into the blood like a fever and leaves the gambler a nervous wreck so far as building a home is concerned. Some homes are being wrecked by children who forget the hands that fed them, and fly the roost too soon to make their own way, without cherishing the love and affection of the mother and father who gave them birth. A home takes years to build, but you can wreck it in one day's carelessness.

It is easier, again, to tear other people apart than it is to put ourselves together. How adept we are at finding fault with the lady across the street, or adversely criticising the cousin in California. Every day, in every town of this world, personalities are being ripped apart by unthinking criticism that is more venomous than curative. Born of jealousy or inferiority or sheer want of something better to do, it is safe to say that all the lights of the world could be lighted with the energy that goes into needless and often untrue tearing down of other people, when our more proper business is putting ourselves together. When I begin to look at myself as critically as I look at my neighbors, then something good can begin to be built within me. When I see my own faults for what they are as clearly as I see the faults of other people, then I can begin to build instead of wreck. Gather in any social circle, from afternoon tea in the mansion house to the bicker session in the country store, and the same usual business is in order, let's tear something down. We all know what is wrong with Hitler, but we cannot think of anything that is wrong with us. We all know about Japan's mistakes, but we cannot remember our own. We all know how the President should run the country, but we cannot quite discover how to run our own lives, personally, day by day.

And the reason is clear, it is harder work to build than it is to tear down, and most of us run around hard work whenever we see an escape.

Over near Copley Square the foundations for a new office building were being set deep in the blue clay of the Back Bay. At the side of the excavation was an observation gallery where visitors could sit and watch the building. The observatory was heated, but it was cold outside. Yet the sidewalk engineers, ensconced in their idle comfort, could make more suggestions for the erecting of that building and the running of the American government than I could jot down while I listened. "Look how slow that man with the pickax is working, and he's probably getting good pay, too." The man who makes that remark is sitting in a warm booth doing nothing. The next comment, "Now that steam shovel has to stand idle until the next truck gets around. Rather poor timing, that." Such comment makes no allowance for the complex intricacies of the traffic around Copley Square, and comes from a man who is expert at tearing down the work other people are trying to do, but makes no effort to build up his own personality and do his own work well.

Yea, verily, it is easier to tear down a house than it is to build one.

When we come to face it, most of us are in one business or the other, house wrecking, or house building. The total effect of our living and talking and working, the end result of the kind of persons we are, is to tear life down around us, or to build it up. And whichever it is, for each of us, the judgment of God is upon us.

Are you in the housewrecking business, or the building trade?

WAYS OF SAYING THANK YOU

WE LIVE in a world where gratitude is not one of the dominant moods. So, first, we had better find something to say Thank You for. Let's begin with the house or hut or palace we live in, right now; the little room only, perhaps, you have to call your own. Thank God for that, even if you still owe last week's rent money. Look around the dear four walls right now, covered with newspapers or satin tapestry, and be glad for a shelter that holds out the cold wind. So often we pray for a house in the country or beg God to let us live somewhere else than where we do, when perchance the place where we are is the place God can use us. Emerson says, you remember, "Every ship looks romantic except the one you are sailing on." So often other people's houses look more romantic than our own. But if you owned that big palace up on the hill, you might not like having to pay taxes on its high valuation, and you might not enjoy the cost of fuel for so big a place, and on wintry nights when you hear the wind howling around the cornices, you might wish for a cosy room in a crowded place just like the one you have now.

Once upon a time, a man wished to sell his small house on a little lot, so he called in an advertising man to write up a description for the papers. When the advertising man showed his copy to the owner, the owner said, "Wait a minute, that's the kind of place I've wanted all my life. I don't think I'll sell it, after all."

So thank God for the place you live in right now. It does not matter where it is, you can make that spot heaven on earth through your creative imagination and skill.

Some years ago, a poor old man and his wife lived in a shack on the Oklahoma plains. One morning, an engineer came up the path and asked if he could drill a test hole for oil under their kitchen floor. He found a gusher, tapped the oil out by the hundreds of barrels and soon put that couple on Easy Street. One day the old man smiled and said reflectively, "But to think it was under our feet all the time." Thank God for the hidden possibilities right around the place where you live. Not that you will find an oil gusher under your kitchen floor, but you will find a hard job that needs doing within a stone's throw of your front door. You can find loneliness that needs friendship within your own block. You can find a little bit of star dust on your own doorstep.

The next thing most of us can find to thank God for is our trouble. For whether we like it or not, mankind is born to trouble as the sparks fly upward. As Rupert Brooke put it:

> Now God be thanked,
> Who hath matched us with His hour.

And God's hour is almost always an hour of crisis, personal or public. Life is never perfect, and the imperfections of our character and our society are the proving ground of our souls. A Christian gets into trouble to help somebody else get out of trouble. That's what Jesus did. He got into plenty of trouble with the Scribes and Pharisees and Caesar's agents, but because he got into trouble for us our way will be a little easier, though we will have our share of trouble, too. It is not so much that we want to avoid trouble as that we ought to hope to go through it, conquer it, make it do us good, overcome it. You remember in Ibsen's great story of Peer Gynt, whenever Peer Gynt comes to trouble, he sidesteps it as gracefully as he can. He avoids every controversy, pussyfoots on every issue, until at the end of a life of failure, he is wandering in the forest and the leaves seem to speak up and say, "We are words, Peer Gynt, thou should'st have spoken us." And the stones say, "We are deeds, Peer Gynt, thou should'st have performed us."

The plain truth is that almost any time is a time of crisis and trouble. When life is prosperous and calm and easy-going, that is a time of trouble too, only the trouble is in our souls and not in our bodies. Remember the lush 1920's when everything seemed to be going along swimmingly? Everybody had a job, night clubs and country clubs did a land office business. And this easy-going luxury of the 1920's has had something to do with the kind of heartbroken world we live in now. We did not get this way overnight. This has been coming on us in the kind of living we have endorsed and the kind of selfish ideals of "Every man for himself and the devil take the hindmost" which have governed much of the personal, business, and political life of our time. The point is this—let us thank God for trouble that will stab us wide awake and show us our need of something better than we are. Let us thank God for trouble that proves to us how far we have wandered away from God, and if our troubles bring us back to Him in penitence then the trouble will not be a total loss.

But even in a world full of trouble, there is plenty of beauty to be thankful for and we do well to say thank you more often than we do. Gratitude is one of the most rewarding moods the human personality can know. Gratitude for little, almost unnoticed things. Let's say thank you for them. Thank you, God, for books to read, written with such care for us by thousands of thinkers down the ages. Thank you, God, for pictures, painted for us by artists in many times and places, pictures that we can see freely for merely the trouble of going to a museum. Thank you, God, for green grass in summer, fair flowers of unending variety. Thank you, God, for clear skies overhead and stars to keep us humble. Thank you, God, for the first clean white snow of winter and for warm fires in our houses on cold nights. Thank you, God, for sleep that drowns our sorrows in Thy deep peace the long night through. Thank you, God, for music that reminds us of a harmony too lovely for words, music that can cool our fevered brows and bring heaven close to earth. Thank you, God and man, for roads that lead to someone's house, someone who does us good when we go there. Thank you, God, for hot soup on a cold day, for fresh bread with butter on it. Thank you, God, for the laughter of little children playing in the sun, for the friendly smile of an old man who has not grown sour with his years. Thank you for letters the postman brings, and thank you for life, liberty, and the pursuit of happiness, even if we never catch it. Thank you for friendly animals we love, a horse with his nose snuggling into a loving palm to find a lump of sugar, a dog that never asks any questions but seems to know the answers, a cat that gives a living demonstration of serenity. For all good things around us, let us say it very simply, very deeply, thank you.

There is another way to say thank you, and that is to pass on to someone else the gratitude you feel. Emerson says, "Beware of too much good staying long in your own hand, it will fast corrupt. Pay it away quickly in some sort."

Take a child from England into your home for the duration. That's one way to say thank you for a home unbombed in the night of terror.

Another way to say thank you, you have already thought of, inviting people who are more or less alone in the world to your house for Thanksgiving dinner. Your turkey will taste better that way than with only your own kith and kin around the cranberry sauce. You may have to do a little hunting to find the people who are not going home for Thanksgiving, if they have a home to go to, but they may be around the corner working in the store or over at the lodging house.

About the most dramatic story of this Thanksgiving happened the other day when the children in a settlement house voluntarily denied themselves turkey, eating hamburger steak instead, and then they sent the pennies they saved for hungry children of the war. That is thanks with giving, now and forever.

THE TYPEWRITER SPEAKING

Seated one day at my typewriter,
    I was weary and ill at ease;
And my fingers wandered idly
    Over the noisy keys.
I knew not what I was writing,
    Or what I was dreaming there,
For the typewriter wrote this message
    As if from out the air.
(With apologies to The Lost Chord: Sullivan)

" "

THIS quotation mark is the trade-mark of the people who are copies of others. They possess no interest in or power for originality. They live by custom rather than conviction. Always following, they never take the lead. If their trade-mark is a quotation mark, their theme song is, "Everybody's doing it now." That makes it right. And their motto is, "When in Rome do as the Romans do."

Not all the people in Rome did as the Romans did. There were a few, contemptuously called Christians, who refused to bow to the Emperor or go to the circus. They were dipped in oil, hung in Nero's Gardens, set fire to. They burned as lights for Nero's bacchanalian feasts, all because the motto written upon their hearts and across their foreheads was somewhat different, "When in Rome do as Christ would do." The difference was noticeable, both to the Romans and to the Christians.

Every moral copyist who justifies his quotation mark by saying, "When in Rome do as the Romans do," is not using that proverb in its fair context. Saint Augustine took his mother, Monica, from their home city of Milan for a visit to Rome. In Rome the fast day was Friday while in the bishopric of Milan the fast day at that time was Saturday. Augustine was in some doubt as to which day he and his mother should observe. So they observed both days. Upon returning to Milan Augustine visited the bishop, Ambrose, and asked what he would advise in such a dilemma. Ambrose calmly answered, "When in Rome do as the Romans do."

Now that advice holds good for such minor matters as fast days, habits of dress or superficial mannerisms that involve no moral issue or personal compromise. In little things, such as shaking hands when you are in Boston yet politely bowing when you are in the Orient, do as is done where you are at the moment.

But whether you shall be honest or dishonest, clean minded or foul, just or crafty, kind or brutal; decisions like these are not geographical, they are universal and there is only one right way to decide them, whether you are in Rome or Boston or Tallahassee.

People who completely copy the moral tone of their environment, without critical or originative selection and judgment, remind me of the Bermuda chub, a fish which can blend with any background. Like the chameleon, this fish changes its color, protectively, to blend with its surroundings. This is an excellent quality—in a fish.

A human being was meant to have his own color of conviction. A human being was meant to be something more than a ditto machine.

$

This is the trade-mark of the people living for what there is in it. They will do anything, for money. Their popular theme song, when they speak on terms of complete frankness with their lovers or their friends is, "Honey, are you making any money? That's all I want to know."

During the First World War a woman was heard to say at the country club, "I don't care how long this war lasts as long as my husband is making as much money as he is now." That is gold standard patriotism. No matter what the crime or business is, it will be crowded if there is money in it. As crowded as Sutter's Farm in 1849.

Liquor is sold to men and women who already have imbibed too much, because there is money in it. Dope is peddled in secret and in public because there is money in it. Somewhere, sometime, a man in a public office which is properly a public trust will sell his vote, because there is money in it. There are women who will go through all the motions of pretending to be in love with a man, because there is money in it. Food supposed to be pure may be adulterated, because there is money in it. Corporations have been known to falsify expenses and bleed the consumers, monopolize products or services and raise the prices, because there is money in it. Racketeers will threaten, assault and murder if necessary, because there is money in it, for a little while. The United States sold 462,782 tons of scrap iron and steel to Germany in 1938, because there was money in it. Or was it to defend democracy in middle Europe?

?

This is the trade-mark of the people who are forever asking questions but never getting the right answers. They are in perpetual doubt about the universe and what to have for supper. Hesitation, indecision, a question mark, these are the marks of their living. Like Rosalind, they ask eight questions in hurried succession, "What did he do? What said he? How looked he? Wherein went he? Did he ask for me? Where remains he? How parted he with thee? And when shalt thou see him again?" and then add, "Answer me in one word." They expect an easy answer to hard questions, and no easy answer shall be given them.

And one suspects that we are too ready to take easy answers instead of true answers. Abbé Dimnet prepared a book on French grammar giving it the tentative title, *French Grammar Made Clear*. His American publishers revised the title, presumably to get in tune with the American spirit, to *French Grammar Made Easy*.

To every question there is an adequate answer, though that answer may be unpalatable, or it may be temporarily buried in the realms of the so-far unknown.

Where is God? That is a hard question, but if you have looked up at the Jungfrau from Lake Thun's sapphire blue water, if you have watched the sun set over Niagara, if you have seen a new-born baby in its mother's arms, if you have read the judgments of history, you have a fair answer to your question. And that answer should be convincing enough to live and love and work and play by. More detailed answers may well wait for a time. So with other questions.

"What about marriage?" Let two lovers dream and plan together, build their house upon the rock, stand together through fair weather and foul, and they have their answer in the far reaches of their hearts.

Why am I alive? That question gets a fair answer when the questioner looks far enough outside of himself to see a hard job that needs doing. He may go, like Kagawa, to the depressed poor of the slums, or like Schweitzer, to the poor sick of Africa, or like Jane Addams, to the riff-raff of Chicago. But with open eyes and hand ready, anyone who will can get a good answer to the question, "Why am I alive?"

$$\frac{1}{2}$$

This is the trade-mark of the people who are only half alive. They are all body, or almost all soul, and they never thus become a whole personality, an integer, 1.

But being half dead is more tragic than being all dead. Trying to live with one foot in the grave and the other on the sidewalk is no fun. I would rather attend my own funeral than take up space half dead, half alive.

For death, complete and irrevocable, has its compensations. You lay down your heavy, earth-soiled burdens.

But this half death, this being part of the person God meant us to be, this neglect of the abundant life Jesus wanted us to live, this is the tragedy.

Easter itself is a trumpet call to the half dead to wake up and live. Easter declares the importance of living. Life, radiant with color and harmony and enthusiasm and purpose, that is what Easter is all about. It is meant to help somebody pull one foot out of the grave and start walking briskly again.

The half hearted are half dead. Let all such become whole-hearted about something or someone. Let affection and love blossom like the magnolia in May. People are to be cherished for what they are, not for what they can do for us.

To be half witted is to be half dead. And any one
of us is half witted when he sees only one side of a
question and refuses to learn the other side and understand it.

Blessed are the all alive, for they shall be saved
from the tragedy of half death.

!

This is the trade-mark of the people who live affirmatively instead of interrogatively. They live by a
few certainties, if need be, instead of in the fog of
their doubts. You will notice that the average typewriter has no exclamation mark on its keyboard. So
it has to be made by putting a period under an
apostrophe. That means we take a simple statement
of fact, and make it our own, to live affirmatively,
with exclamation. Here are a few simple statements
of fact, any one of which, if made personally regnant
in any life, will make that life more full of exclamation than question.

"People are more important than things."

"I shall believe the best about people and about
life."

"Over the years we reap what we sow."

"There is something in the world for me to do. I
shall find it."

"Kindness is the greatest power in the world."

Two other keys on the typewriter are trade-marks.

One is the Back Spacer. It is the trade-mark of the people who think there were no times like the good old days. Everything used to be right, now nothing is as nice as it was then. Even a superficial reading of history will make clear that the Golden Nineties were not golden for the millions who suffered definite poverty with very little private or government interest in their Stygian darkness. Romantic memories have a way of dropping out the brutal realities of the past.

The Margin Release is the trade-mark of the people who find it impossible to keep within bounds in the little game of life. They insist on stepping over the edge. There is plenty of room within the law for creative imagination to find full scope. Stepping over the edge of the laws of reason or the laws of God is an overworking of the Margin Release. When the bell rings in the conscience, it is time to stop and think.

This is what the typewriter says.

THE WINTER'S FIRST SNOW

FROM a window on Beacon Street at midnight I watched the white miracle of Boston's first snowstorm. We are all tired of the slushy, dirty stuff before March comes, but the first snow is as much of a sheer joy to grandmother as to grandson. Coming in the middle of the night, as this storm did, gives it a romance that snow in the daytime never has. At midnight the world is hushed and the snow makes it more hushed. The whiteness glistens in reflection from the twinkling street lights.

And what a joy it is to see the dark alleyways covered over with a blanket of pristine whiteness. Dirty things are out of sight now for a little, and the world is washed whiter than snow, or at least as white. Ugly bumps and angles take on graceful white curves. Bare trees assume the semblance of fairyland and ordinary human beings become ethereal ghosts. Every lane is a great white way and even the ash cans in the backyard are not unlovely with their caps of white fur. The fences wear an ermine fringe and every cornice and wall has grown in height and beauty with its load of snow crystals.

Out of the stilly night a train whistles in the far

away, trying to plow its way through the gathering drifts to a waiting station and quiet rest after labor. Soon the snowplows rumble along the street to break a way through for the morning traffic; then the milkman stumbles through the yard while his suddenly white horse stands by at the gate.

On the dark Charles River the snow makes not the slightest impression, melting and merging into the water course from whence it came. How many ages past this thing, called water, has been going through its unending cycle. The river flows to the sea and on some sunny day a steamy vapor rises from off the ocean to make the cloud. That cloud floats back with the northeast wind, over the land, and falls in rain or snow on the Charles River watershed. Many days later that drop of water, soaking through the soil, finds its way to a brooklet on Big Blue Hill. That brook flows into a creek, that creek into a rivulet, that rivulet into the Charles and the Charles flows on to the ocean again and the whole thing starts over.

A snowstorm does a lot of things to us that are good for us. For one thing it makes us appreciate warm houses on a blustery night. I suppose that life in the luxurious South Seas is idyllic and balmy, but one point is certain, easy-going year-round warmth is not too good for the coal companies nor for the vigor of the human mind and soul. Anthropologists leave no doubt about the fact that our rigorous climate produces a mental activity which is the source of much of our invention and cultural progress. Not that the world shows much progress in the art of living together, but we trust this is the dark before the dawn, the end of an age of terror and the beginning of an age of wisdom.

And another good result of a snowstorm is the way it makes us help each other in a hard place. Strangers who never think of speaking to one another in good weather pitch in and help a fellow out of a snow drift. Pedestrians jokingly give a shove to a wallowing truck with a heigh-ho and a cheery blow. It's always good weather when good fellows get together in a snowstorm. Grumbling about the inconvenience of it all just does not go in a snowstorm. Everybody takes it as a joke, and the more the trouble, the bigger the joke. That kind of philosophy is worth developing, even if it takes a snowstorm to do it. Friends over from England tell us the same kind of helping each other out of trouble holds true in an air raid, although that is no joke like a snowstorm. Whenever unaccustomed danger strikes, that is when deep-going character shows itself for what it is, the real thing or only veneer.

Another good thing a snowstorm does for us is to break up our little pet paths of routine activity. We have to change gears for once; nobody gets to work quite as easily as usual; we have to walk around the corner instead of through a drift, over mounds of snow and through unshovelled walks. We have to pause to let somebody else come through the narrow path. At the office everybody has a different story of how he or she got to work. Now this jarring us loose from too habitual ways is a good thing once in a while. Once I met a man in San Francisco who extolled the weather in that fair city by saying, "It's like this all year round, no change of seasons. I never have to wear an overcoat." He thought that was high praise for the weather around the Golden Gate. I thought then how some of us would miss the winter's first snowstorm if it never came. We come to like and look for the change of seasons. How could you and I live without the first crocuses of spring along the Avenue, or the fragrant June nights when the fireflies make sport? Or how would we live without the first crisp day of autumn when the leaves start to color? These changes of seasons with their concomitant changes of routine are the very elixir of life to millions of human beings.

Something else the snowstorm tells us is that each of us must keep his own sidewalk clean. The snowplow will take care of the public street but you and I have to take care of our own sidewalks. Right at the curbstone private and public morality meet and coalesce. I am responsible for my little stretch of walk and my neighbor is responsible for his and the city is responsible for the public highway. We each have our job to do. But good manners dictate that I shovel a little bit of my neighbor's walk, and all of it if he is sick or out of town, rather than hew to the line too closely.

Then, too, a snowstorm is a great test of patience.

With long lines of traffic waiting to break through the snow-piled streets, any motorist who can keep sweet in snow-stalled traffic has passed with a high mark a test in patience.

It seems hard to believe, but it must be true, that every snow crystal that ever has or ever will fall upon the earth beneath is designed in a hexagonal shape. Never five-sided, never seven-sided, always six-sided, with intricate lacework patterns. Study a snowflake carefully while it rests on your coat sleeve and gain a new respect for the infinite detail which God puts into the creation of something so small and so short-lived. Be it a paramecium, or an atom, or a mustard seed, or a snowflake, God is a skilled craftsman.

These afternoons the children are having the time of their lives. Stop to watch their carefree coasting, listen in on their happy chatter and their easy-going banter. You will not hear a word about bombs over Europe. They do not say much about blockades and embargoes. That is all to the good. Spare them the grimness of a world at war if we can, for their child-hood years. Let them coast in peace and jollity, while they may, and may they do so for a long time to come. Six husky youngsters crowd on one toboggan and off they go to crash into a snowbank and tumble over each other in the whirling white powder. How they love it! Then the long walk back up the hill. They remind us of a Chinaman's definition of a toboggan ride, "Whish, walk a mile!"

Literature has many stories and poems which

glorify snow as their central theme. There is the fantastic tale of Baron Munchausen in which he tells of the traveler who became lost in a snowstorm but finally tied his horse to a lone fence post in a wilderness of white, while he, the traveler, lay down in the snow to rest. While he slept the snow melted and in the morning he found himself asleep on a church lawn. Looking about for his horse, he found him tied to the top spire of the church steeple.

Another pointed snow story from somewhere relates that a father, hiking through deep snow, suddenly turned around to see his son stretching his little legs to keep in his father's footsteps. Whereupon the father said to himself, "If that boy is going to follow in my footsteps, I guess I'd better make tracks for heaven."

Thank God for the winter's first snow.

AN OUNCE OF PREVENTION

FROM my window I see a tattered, bedraggled cloth sign hanging limply from a lamp post. In faded letters it says, "This is Fire Prevention Week." I am glad somebody left that sign up, long after Fire Prevention Week is supposed to be over, because that sign makes a good text.

For fire prevention should never be over. If your cellar is full of combustible rubbish, clean it out tomorrow morning. If old electric wires in your house may be crossed and ready to short circuit, tear off the wall paper and straighten out those wires right soon. But not only is fire prevention a text on a lamp post. There is an excellent correlative text in the Bible when James reminds us, "How great a matter a little fire kindleth."

One summer in California I drove for half a day through thick smoke hanging like a pall over the landscape. On the distant hills, covered with dry forests, a snarling, voracious fire swept unchecked for days, burning out millions of dollars worth of lumber and endangering human life. A careless match dropped by a hunter in the mountains had set off that blaze. Indeed, what a great matter a little fire kindleth.

The fire chief in your town will tell you that the safety of your home from devastating fire depends far more on the preventive action of thousands of common people than it does on the cure of a few fire engines. An ounce of prevention always has been worth a pound of cure. Building a house that is fireproof is far wiser than depending too much on the firemen after the fire has started.

So crime prevention, by all odds, is more important and more needed than the cure of crime after the crime is committed. It is essential to our common happiness that we try to keep our children out of crime in the first place, instead of trying to punish them after they get into crime in the second place. An ounce of prevention is worth a pound of cure.

I want right here to pay my respects to the Police Department for the way they handle the threat of widespread crime on Hallowe'en. The hoodlum, hobgoblin, break-in and bust-it spirit runs wild on a night like that and the police know it full well. So what do they do, call out the reserves and stand at every corner with a night stick poised in air ready to come down on the first recalcitrant head that pokes its way into trouble? Not a bit of it. The police of Boston know the expulsive power of a new affection, so they invited all the children of the city to come around to the police stations at 8 P.M. and have a Hallowe'en Party with the officers as their hosts. I stopped around at Station 16 on Boylston Street to see how this prevention would work out. Standing on the lower step, right under that usually terrifying blue light, was Officer Stockdale, ushering the costumed children into the station like a father welcoming home a long lost child. And the children were trooping up the station stairs as if they were entering a fairy palace. I climbed the stairs and there on the second floor were four hundred happy, singing, shouting children ranging in age from little ones, hardly able to walk, up to boys big enough to make a lot of trouble outdoors if the devil got into them. At a table at the side, big, burly officers were handing out free lunches and soft drinks to the pop-eyed youngsters. And up front an Irish officer was leading the singing as if his job depended on it. On a small table near the door rested the bean blowers and rocks and ripe fruit that some of the ragamuffins had intended to use that night. But they checked their missiles at the door and forgot to call for them when they went home.

Any normal boy has to have outlet for his energy. If we do not give him a chance to play in a playground, if we do not give him a chance to make things with his hands at a workbench, if we do not help him form a scout troop or club where he can be with his natural friends, then his energy will break out somewhere else and he will be in a gang hell-bent for getting their excitement somewhere, even if it has to be outside the law. "Satan finds work for idle hands to do," is true of children as well as of adults. Fathers and mothers, are we doing as good a job of prevention as the policemen of Boston? I wonder.

Turn now, if you will, to the importance of sickness prevention, in a day when so much money and energy are spent on sickness cures. Surely we need doctors to cure us after the disease gets started. But even more than that, we need common sense to make us live so that many of our sicknesses never will get started. How many of us are eating and drinking in moderation at Sunday dinner time? How many of us will get out of the house, at three o'clock, for a brisk walk around the park or over the hill or down to the shore or even just around the long block? Some of us will never forget the cleansing power, the fresh reviving of that Sunday afternoon walk with father to talk to, or a friend closer than a brother, to understand. One of the sad results of an automobile age is our growing inability to walk for health's sake. An ounce of preventive exercise is worth a pound of curative medicine.

And what shall we say of accident prevention as being surely as important as the ambulance that sirens its way cross-town when prevention is too late? Out on the Newburyport Turnpike is the newest gadget in accident prevention. It is a traffiscope set at the top of a hill, a set of mirrors on a framework over the road so that you can see over the hill and know what is coming. It is obviously a great help in accident prevention, although it is still wise to keep to the right going over a hill, mirrors or no mirrors. My son brought home from school the other day a Red Cross list of preventive measures which all of us can take at home. Are the stairs free of packages which might cause a bad fall? Are the floors slippery? Are poisons put out of reach of children? Are you sure that gun is unloaded? Accidents do not have to happen. They happen because they are caused, usually by somebody's carelessness. An ounce of prevention is worth a ton of cure, right here.

I wonder if it would do any good to have a Divorce Prevention Week. We could start with less marrying in haste and repenting at leisure. Three questions honestly asked of themselves by two people who are in love would prevent more divorces than you could shake a stick at. The first question is, "Do we know each other's faults and still love each other?"

A second question which would prevent some divorces is this, "Do we both have the same basic ideals of character and conduct so that we can trust each other to be loyal to what we both believe?" If there is a wide difference in what makes for honor and truth, then there is trouble ahead. A third question which two people, thinking of getting married, could well ask is this, "Will trouble draw us closer together or drive us farther apart?" If it looks like a fair weather marriage with success riding only through the sunshine, then it may not hold, because sooner or later any marriage comes to rough water when a delicate sense of balance and courage will be greatly needed to keep the thing from being swamped. An ounce of prevention is worth a pound of cure.

In the last place, now that we are all looking desperately for a cure for war, and the fire engines of war are clanging over the earth, let us try to keep some little corner of our minds and souls for the cultivation of a preventive for war. When this war is cured, if ever in our time, what will prevent the next one, more terrible than the last? That is a long-time question but it is an important one. What about overpopulation as a cause of war? What about poor treaties? What about starvation tariffs? What about the control of economic resources? What about a world government? Here are questions that will have to be answered before we find a preventive for war. But how we do need it!

And remember that prevention is always quieter, less sensational than cure. The cure is often as dramatic as the old fire engine with its three white horses and belching smoke and sparks. But prevention is quiet and painstaking and unsensational. So a cure for cancer will be dramatic and startling, but the preventive is slow moving and will not get such black headlines. So it always has been, so it always will be, but even so, an ounce of prevention will be worth at least a pound of cure.

COURAGE IN QUEER PLACES

FROM my window I see the Charles River, frozen over with a sheet of glassy ice. But do not try to skate on that treacherous glass, for it is too thin to be safe. One of the few sorrows of the long winter is the long casualty list of children who have fallen through thin ice, some to be rescued just in the nick of time, others, alas, to be lost forever, unless their heart-broken parents meet them, perchance, in a better world.

I saw courage on the Charles River the other day, and I must tell you about it.

Motoring along the River Drive near Harvard College, I saw a group of excited boys at the edge of the ice waving to something out in the middle of the stream. Drawing up to the curb and walking down to see the excitement, it became clear that a huge police dog had fallen through the ice and was struggling desperately to get back to shore. Some fool boy had thrown a stick out on the ice and the poor dog, not knowing the danger, ran after the stick, to his quick downfall on thin ice!

Nobody knew what to do. The dog swam frantically from side to side of the small open hole in the center of the icy river. He tried to crawl up on the ice, but the ice broke under his weight and he floundered under water again, struggled up and tried again. Time after time the ice broke under his weight, or he put his paws on the sharp edges, unable to pull himself out. Of course he grew weaker with each vain struggle. None of us on shore dared venture out on the ice alone, because it would surely break under our weight and then there would be one more victim to rescue.

Soon men with ladders appeared and tried laying them end to end toward the fast weakening dog. But there were not enough ladders to reach that far.

How our hearts ached for that brave dog. By now he knew he could not save himself, so he began looking toward the shore, barking in feeble voice for help we could not think of.

Now came the right answer—a policeman with a small rowboat. Wheeling it to the edge of the river, he quickly slid it out over the more solid ice until suddenly the boat broke through into the water and the brave policeman got the ducking of his life in the cold water. But he struggled over the stern of that little boat and climbed in, then broke through the remaining ice and at last came within reach of the panting, almost hopeless, almost dead but courageous police dog who would not give up and sink. The policeman lifted that poor creature out of the icy water, then struggled back through the broken floes to shore.

There was hardly a dry eye on the shore that cold morning as the dog shook himself partially dry and leaped up on the shoulders of the boy who was obviously his beloved owner. Within the minute, he was wagging his tail and had evidently forgiven whoever it was that threw the stick in that foolish direction.

We all read stories about courage, but it is seldom that we see the thing and know it when we see it for what it is, sheer bravery against overwhelming odds. Rescues, like this, of animals and what are more precious, children, have happened all over New England each winter. And today I take off my hat to the courage of the rescued and the rescuers.

Speaking of courage in animals, I once saw bravery in a little mouse which I shall not soon forget. I call this story courage in a bath tub. On this particular evening somebody cornered a mouse in the bathroom, and the chase was on. In the midst of the wild excitement, the clever mouse scrambled along the water pipes and jumped into the bath tub. That meant we could catch him easily, so I reached in to capture him, but that mouse eluded my grasp and darted for the drain pipe, then disappeared into the darkness of the plumbing system, like Jean Valjean hiding in the sewers of Paris. We gave that foolish mouse up for dead and forgot about him.

But we forgot too soon. Two days after the wild chase, somebody gave the alarm and called the household to visit the bathroom again and look into the tub. That mouse had come back from the grave. Wet, thin, shivering, fearful, beady-eyed, so weak he was almost dead, that brave mouse had withstood the flooding of rivers of bath water. He had hunted a way of escape up and down the pipes of the plumbing system, and failing to find a way out into light and air, he had traced his way back to the bath tub whence he had started his desperate adventure.

Always before I had looked upon mice as rather unnecessary vermin, put here upon earth in a moment when God could not have been minding his business. But now, looking down upon courage in that bath tub, I changed my mind, at least momentarily, for I had seen what everyone admires, anywhere, any time, the will to live, bravery, courage, in the face of almost certain annihilation.

You will ask what I did about that mouse? I did not have the heart to kill him, so I gathered him up and carried him out into the warm sunshine, laid his fragile little body in the warmest, grassiest spot I could find, and left him to his destiny. I do not think he lived long, he was so weak, but if his body is now in the grave of this, our earth, I am sure that his little soul is resting in peace somewhere in that mouse heaven which I am sure God has ready for those who will not give up, even unto the least of these, the mouse.

So far I have been talking about courage in animals. Now let us think about courage in people, people who break through the ice and almost drown spiritually, people who get lost in the dark wilderness of their despair and try desperately to find their way back to life. The woods and the cities too are full of courage, most of it so quiet you hardly guess its presence.

For there are two kinds of courage. Physical courage shows itself in the man who risks his personal safety to help somebody else, or even to save himself. But then there is also moral courage, the kind which risks popularity to be right, to be found standing for the hard truth against the easy lie. Moral courage faces a long illness without whimpering. Moral courage faces subtle, powerful temptations without losing personal honor or integrity. Moral courage knows when to say yes and when to say no. Moral courage does not ask, "What is everybody else doing?" but, "What ought I to do about this?"

Moral courage means daring to be different from the crowd if being different means being right.

Do you have this kind of priceless courage? Only the testing time will tell. La Rochefoucauld puts it this way, "The man who has never been in danger cannot answer for his courage."

Sooner or later each one of us will face a dangerous situation, dangerous to our bodies or dangerous to our souls. What we do when that time comes will decide whether or not we have any courage at all, either physical or moral.

Sometimes people who keep up their courage when things look dark are laughingly accused of "Whistling in the dark." Another version of the same so-called weakness is this: "He's whistling past the cemetery."

Far from being foolish, whistling in the dark is about the best thing a man can do. Certainly there is no better way to pass a cemetery. You can walk a mile around the cemetery, if you are afraid of it, but there is more courage in whistling past it.

Whistling in the dark, that is the bravest thing you can do, because your very assumed cheer will make you feel better and drive away the fantasies of the night, so many of which are imaginary, at best.

In 1868 a young medical student in Philadelphia by the name of Edward Trudeau came down with tuberculosis. His classmates said that was the end of him. But he began to whistle in the dark. Conserving the little strength he had left, he studied medicine again and graduated. Thin and worn, he had to be taken to the Adirondacks in a wagon. As the woodsmen carried him into the hunting lodge one remarked, "Why, doctor, you don't weigh no more than a dried lambskin." For thirty-nine years Dr. Trudeau stayed right there, not to die, but to find a new life, a life which founded the Saranac Hospital for tuberculosis, a life which made the first pioneering discoveries concerning the treatment of the white plague. Before Dr. Trudeau, the rule had been, "Keep the windows shut and don't let in the sun." Dr. Trudeau exposed the foolishness of that idea and he exposed the patients to sunlight, with healing power. Out of the wild mountain forests he built cottages, starting with only a farmhouse for a hospital and two poor factory girls as patients. Now the whole village of Saranac centers around what Dr. Trudeau did. Given up for dead, he insisted on living. Almost buried in the cemetery, he began to whistle in the dark, and thousands have been healed by his whistling. That is courage, courage of the highest order, courage of the kind I cherish, and wish for you and me.

For wherever you meet it, courage is worth the respect of every man.

THE SPICE OF LIFE

FROM my window I watched a truck stop for a red light the other day and on that truck was an address that stabbed me wide awake, 18 Spice Street. Now I had not happened to know that there was a Spice Street in Boston, so when I saw that romantic name I could almost smell the cinnamon and the cloves and the nutmeg, right through my window. An overpowering desire to visit Spice Street swept over me and so, the next time I found myself driving my car I was on my way through the crooked downtown lanes of Boston, asking the traffic cops, "Where is Spice Street?" It must be near the water front.

I found it, and as good luck would have it, there was a spice factory right on the corner of Spice Street, just as it should be. And the discovery of Spice Street reminds us of the spice of life.

There is a pretty spice story for children about a Chinese boy named Pun Kee who did not like ginger, but wherever he went people were eating ginger and he was quite unhappy, until he happened upon a ginger factory and discovered that in a ginger factory nobody eats ginger, and the smell becomes so familiar they do not notice it. So Pun Kee, who did not like ginger, lived happily ever after, working in a ginger factory.

Which is another way of saying that spice is something that is to be taken in small parcels, if it is to be enjoyed. Too much spice is too much. I noticed in this spice factory that all the spices are put up in very small packages. You do not buy a pound of cinnamon, you buy a few ounces at a time.

And that is as it should be with another kind of spice, called the spice of life. A little should go a long way. But when a man thinks spice is the main dish and forgets that it is only a seasoning for other substantial foodstuffs, then something goes wrong with that man's life.

Life is principally soup and potatoes and rice pudding with an occasional steak if you are lucky. Life is not principally nutmeg and cayenne and mustard. Mustard alone is a rather unpleasant diet. But what mustard and cayenne and nutmeg and pepper can do is to bring out the flavor of other more prosaic foods.

Now it is right here that the spice of life is like the spice of the East Indies, it should give flavor and aroma and charm to the more prosaic business of everyday living, and the spice should never be an end in itself. Some of the unhappiest people I know are those who are trying to live on spice without the rice pudding under it, and the human soul cannot stand that kind of diet any more than the human stomach can.

To idle away the months of the winter on the

beaches of Florida and to idle away the months of summer in Maine is to live a life which is so over-done with spice that it cannot be tasted for what it is worth. The plain everyday rice pudding of down-right hard work has been forgotten. Not many of us can forget the work. But whenever somebody does live on spices, be sure of this, it is not as much fun as it seems to be. People come to the place where they cannot taste the spice they live with all the time.

The next thing I notice about the spice trade is that our spices are about the most international prod-ucts we use; they come from almost everywhere on earth except our own country. We, in America, pro-duce only a small part of the mustard and chili pep-pers used in the spice business. Nutmeg comes from Granada in the West Indies, cloves from romantic Zanzibar on the east coast of Africa, paprika from Hungary, coriander and pepper from India, cinna-mon from Ceylon, ginger and mustard from China, mace and white pepper from Sumatra and Singapore and Borneo.

A hundred years ago these spices came to America in the swift sailing clippers of Salem, and now they come in less romantic freighters. Look at that pepper shaker in front of you as you eat your Sunday dinner. That pepper probably grew in a grove in India, came out along a jungle road in an ox-cart, found itself at Bombay where a steamer picked it up and brought it to Boston, then over to Spice Street where it was freshly ground, packed and sent to your grocer. And pepper today comes to you a little cleaner than it used to. A clipper ship, years ago, was known to leave India with a cargo of hides below decks and a cargo of pepper in casks above decks. As the hides settled in the hold, the pepper was poured in loose for ballast, to fill in the chinks and crannies among the hides. Old timers say that pepper used to have a rarer flavor in those good old days!

However times may have changed, it is still true that almost the whole earth comes to our table bringing spices. So too, our cultural life is enriched by treasures from the whole earth. We read Tolstoi's essays out of Russia. We listen to Sibelius' music out of Finland; we look at da Vinci's pictures out of Italy; we read Tagore's poetry out of India; we quote Lin Yutang, out of China; we read Don Quixote by Cervantes out of Spain; we treasure Goethe's Faust out of Germany; we gaze with wonder upon Corot's landscapes out of France. So then, not only the spice on our table, but the spice of our life is an international business, knowing no boundaries of inspiration. This is just as it should be, and let us live and hope for the day when we recognize ourselves as children of the whole earth, owing the whole earth our thanks for what we have and are. Within a long stone's throw of my window is a statue of William Lloyd Garrison, with this inscription under it, "My country is the world, my countrymen all mankind."

It was William Cowper who coined the phrase you have been thinking of while I have been talking, "Variety is the spice of life." What I have been saying up to now I have said to the point that this spice of variety can be overdone, and that life is mainly a business of plain food rather than spice.

Now let me speak to those of you who have precious little variety in life, who, far from being sated with the aroma of spice, hardly know what the flavors are, because they seem expensive and quite out of reach.

One inexpensive spice is good reading. "There is no frigate like a book to take you miles away." And an even better idea is to gather a few of your friends together to read aloud any good book. I know a group in Concord which meets evenings to read Emerson's essays aloud. Try that little spice, if your days are filled with dull routine.

Another tasty spice, in small doses, is an evening of games around the parlor table. Some of us remember, almost with nostalgia, the parchesi, authors, and "Ask me another" games of our childhood. And God help any child who has to live through endless evenings of Dad behind the newspaper and Mother deep in her sewing basket. "Let's play a game" is the healthiest cry for a little spice that ever rose from the lips of a bored grandson or grandmother in a house where the grim business of living has been grim too long and needs a little spice to flavor the rice pudding.

Have you discovered your spice of life?

FACES

FROM my window I see faces passing in endless procession; gay faces, sad faces, plain faces, made-up faces. Where do they come from, where do they go? What deep thoughts do the faces hide or reveal? Has this face changed in the last year? I suppose I am a very rude and overbearing and impertinent man, but I never tire of trying to fathom the faces of the people who come near enough for me to see. Faces are like little books, if you know how to read them.

Now mark you, I am not claiming that every face is a complete revelation of the character behind the face. That would be a ridiculous assumption. Physiognomy, the study of character from facial expression, is a suspect, charlatan science, and I dare not defend it too stoutly. In 1743 the English Parliament passed a law forbidding the practice of physiognomy because quacks tried to tell the future in clients' faces just as a palmist tries to read the future in the palm of the hand. This is dangerous business at best. Here is fair warning from the poet Moore:

> In vain we fondly strive to trace
> The soul's reflection in the face;
> In vain we dwell on lines and crosses,

Crooked mouths and short probosces;
Boobies have looked as wise and bright
As Plato and the Stagyrite
And many a sage and learned skull
Has peeped through windows dark and dull.

It is so. Character does not often put its finest goods
in the show window of the face. We all know men
who look like prize fighters and carry Phi Beta Kappa
keys on their watch chains. There are women with
faces like angels whose manners are not angelic, to
put it mildly.

Faces can be deceiving, but they can also be reveal-
ing. For one face that tells a lie about the character
behind it, nine other faces tell the approximate truth.
There is something in this physiognomy business,
and it would not be amiss for all of us to read character better than we do. We might save ourselves serious mistakes and help people to understand themselves. Aristotle began clarifying the facts which faces
reveal, and his work has been carried on by Havelock
Ellis and Charles Darwin and other men of sound
scientific repute.

But let us approach the thing very simply today.
For instance, we all admit that a quick emotion, like
fear, is quickly revealed in the face. The eyes almost
pop out of the head, the skin turns pale, so that one
look at a face like that convinces anybody that fear
is the cause. So, in greater or less degree, many of our
emotional and physical states are recorded in our
facial expression.

Take hunger, you cannot keep that out of your face very long. But most of you who read this book have never seen a face hollowed and drawn by long-continued hunger. There are not many such people around our well-fed New England towns and countryside, today, thank God. But there may be more than we guess. It is not far in a straight line from where you live to where somebody's face shows leanness because the cupboard is bare. The relief money, if there is any, does not buy enough milk for the five children, and good meat and plenty of vegetables are scarce. In the heart of our crowded cities there is more starvation than we ever guess because we do not go down to see it—it might make us sick.

And then there is the sharecropper who does not get a fair share of the crop. In debt to the owner before he starts to harvest the cotton or the corn, he pays high interest rates and buys his supplies at high prices in the owner's store. In a world which could produce plenty, and does, food rots on the ground because we cannot think up a system to get surplus food into people's stomachs to fill out the faces of hungry human beings.

And if there are faces lean with hunger right here on our own doorstep, think of what it is in Belgium and Holland and the other conquered countries of Western Europe, not to mention the forty million famine-famished bodies with souls, trying to hang on, in China. There are a lot of lean faces on the earth today. Mothers with little children in China are throwing themselves into the rivers after the last measure of rice is gone and no more food of any kind in sight. Western Europe is feeling the starvation after the harvests were trampled under the heel of the enemy. It is not a very sunshiny thing to say, but I think it is true, that today in this upset world more faces are lean with hunger than ever before in the history of civilization. The cave man did better for his family with his stone ax and strong right arm than we do with tractors and complicated systems of economic maldistribution.

But if hunger gets into a face, so does gluttony, its opposite. When we over-indulge in food or drink, and keep up that over-indulgence through the years, the story gets into the face as surely as night follows day. The florid, flabby face is the written record of what we have done.

Or worry, how that nightmare writes its lines in deep furrows on the brow between the eyes and sags the whole face into its tragedy. Not one person in ten can keep his worry out of his face. As Goldsmith phrased it, "Well had the boding tremblers learned to trace the day's disasters in his morning face." Mothers worrying about their boys away at camp or out after midnight, how it shows on their faces. Wives worried about their children out after dark or about their husbands away from home when they should be home. How a wife's worry can get into her face. Strong men worried about their business and how long it will hold together, how that worry can write itself on the face. We often think we hide worry, but more than we guess, it shows itself, and other people, loath to tell, keep their observations to themselves. But they see more than they say.

Or take treachery and deceit, they have a way of getting into our faces against all our efforts to be poker face. Treachery will make the eye shifty and the face muscles nervous, often such slight alterations that we think they are unobserved. But someone who loves us and knows us can tell that something is wrong. We cannot fool everybody forever.

But already I hear someone saying that his or her face is a misfortune, so homely that nothing can help it. Yes, something can, and that something is more than you buy in a cosmetic shop. You remember the lines in Hamlet, "God has given you one face and you make yourselves another." And the resultant face that the world sees is a combination of that face God gave us, mingled with the face we make for ourselves by our inner thoughts and our daily conduct. And the face we make can visibly alter the face God gave us, believe it or not.

Here is a woman with a face as plain as a board fence, as they say. But her inner spirit is so radiant with the light of love, or religion, that glory shines out through that face and the little world around her is glad for the blessing of her presence. As Longfellow said, "The light upon her face shines from the windows of another world." We know what that means, because we know people like that. The face

God gave them was nothing extra, but the face they have made for themselves by inner radiance is worth walking a mile to see. That radiance is not skin deep and does not lose its lustre with the passing years.

The best kind of face-lifting we ever do is done when high inner character breaks out into a straight-forward countenance that can look people squarely in the eye and show the friendliness that is not pretended. Our faces, over the years, do reveal the quality of our thoughts, the conduct of our days. There is no fairer picture on earth than the animation and glory of a plain face, grown uncommonly lovely with inner discipline and patience and courage and courtesy. There is no sadder picture on earth than the God-given face of beauty decaying into common commonness by the vacuity and shallowness of the mind and soul behind it. The question is not, what kind of face did God give you? The prior question is this, what kind of face are you making for yourself now? We all wish for a face like Helen of Troy's that launched a thousand ships. But do not forget that face launched also a thousand troubles and heart breaks and regrets. As Marlowe adds, that face launched the ships and also burnt the topless towers of Ilium.

But whatever got me started talking about faces? I will tell you. At the Boston Museum of Fine Arts, I have seen an exhibition of portraits covering forty-five centuries, from an Egyptian Prince of 3000 B.C. down to Jo Davidson's head of a New Englander done in 1935. Here were the faces of people—Chinese, Indian, Greek, Roman, European, American. The Museum had carefully gathered together in one place hundreds of these portraits, pictures of human beings. And here was Rembrandt's portrait of his own father. The sadness of the ages is in that man's face, hard work is written on his hands. It is Rembrandt at his best, a lighted face against a dark background. Here also you will see one of El Greco's sensitive faces; also the substantial, realistic faces of the Dutch School. And here you will see the famous Gilbert Stuart portrait of George Washington, pink cheeked and quite unfinished.

And last of all, think of the infinite variety in the human face. How many billions of people have lived on the face of the earth, with no two faces ever exactly alike. How many patterns God must have in his pattern shop. And he never uses the same pattern twice. No one of millions yet unborn will look exactly like anybody who ever has or ever will live.

This infinite variety of face ought to remind us of something, the variety of our minds and souls. No two minds think in exactly the same channels, at least God did not intend that they should. No two souls will have exactly the same identical experience of God and of life.

And what a difference one face, near or far, can make in our happiness.

POWER TO BREAK DOWN OR BUILD UP

I WATCHED a miniature show of free fireworks the other day. The street car tracks on Massachusetts Avenue needed repairing by the welding crew. Six men bring their yellow cart, unbox their welding equipment and set it over the rails. Then they push a long pole up into the air and hook it over the trolley wire to draw their power out of the car line. A man, who looks like a deep sea diver in his helmet and heavy gloves, bends over the work to be done, grasps two carbon rods in his strong hands and then the sparks begin to fly. It is a great show and little boys like me have great fun watching it.

I got so interested I stayed around until the man with the helmet finished his job, then I asked him whether he was welding or cutting. He explained that he had been welding two joints together, then he added, "It's a funny thing, but we use the same power and about the same outfit to weld or to cut; it's just the way you handle the power that makes the difference."

And I want to pass on to you that sermon from a track repair foreman, "We use the same power to put things together or break them apart; it's just the way we handle that power that makes the difference."

Mark this, as human beings and as corporate groups, all of us are handling high power almost all the time, and what we do with that power is what makes the world we live in, private and public, like heaven or hell. That power is like fire, it is either our best friend or our worst enemy. Let power be controlled as fire is in a fireplace or a furnace, then that power can drive our lives and warm our days with radiant good cheer. But let that power get out of control, like a fire that overheats the chimney and sets the whole house ablaze, then there is the devil to pay, and power that should be used to hold things together is now running wild to tear things apart.

Take for instance the power of ambition. We say every boy ought to grow up with a fine streak of ambition in his soul. He ought to be ambitious for himself, he ought to want to come to something, be an honor and a joy to his family. That is true. And ambition like that can hold a boy together and keep him at his studies when he would rather go fishing. Ambition like that will make him take a hard job selling papers or making a garden in order to put himself through school. And when he gets a chance to wait on table at college to pay for his board he will jump at the chance because he has ambition, that electric power that integrates his personality. His life has been welded by a great power.

But that same power of ambition can run wild and raise havoc with a man and all of life around him.

That is what ambition came to be to Macbeth, "Vault-ing ambition, which o'erleaps itself, and falls on the other." Such a man is indeed choked with his ambi-tion and we can understand how Brutus felt when he said of his once much loved Caesar, "There is tears for his love, joy for his fortune, honour for his valour, and death for his ambition."

So it is that when a man steps on other members of his family to try to rise higher on a social scale, when a man who holds ambitions in business feeds those ambitions on the starvation of the men and women and children who earn his dividends for him; when ambition gets into the blood like a fever, then that power is being used to tear life down, not to weld it together. "We use the same power to put things together or break them apart, it's just the way we handle that power that makes the difference." So we are reminded that it was when the angels were ambitious to become equal with God that they fell into the nether regions and became the devil's arch-angels.

Let us have ambition by all means. Life is stale and altogether tasteless without it. But make sure of this—that our ambition is holding life together, not tearing it apart.

Look next, if you will, at the electric power of the thing we call patriotism, love of country. How strong it is to hold a country together or tear the world apart in bloody torture.

Say a prayer of thanksgiving to God every night for

the kind of American patriotism we have which holds this blessed land together under the Stars and Stripes. How lucky we are that for three thousand miles across and a thousand miles from north to south we have one flag, one capital, one national government, one precious country. Of course we have so-called sectionalism; New England often wants things her way in Washington, and the cotton South wants things another way, and the rural midwest puts in an oar for the farmer, but our love of the whole country is so strong that we are willing to yield a little here and sacrifice a bit there in order to keep this country together. If you love your little cottage on the Cape you know also that a gentleman in Georgia loves his plantation house. If you love your white farmhouse in New Hampshire you know that a Navajo Indian loves his hogan in the desert. If you love your cozy apartment on Fifth Avenue you know that somebody else loves his brownstone front on Halsted Street in Chicago. If you love that slum hovel on the third floor back because it is home to you, you can understand how a negro mammy loves her log cabin that lets the wind through the cracks. It is home, sweet home. And we are Americans all. And we are very, very lucky.

But look what happens when patriotism runs wild and o'erleaps the boundaries of common sense. In many countries of the earth today the patriot says something like this: "I love my country so much I want her to be greater than she is. My country needs more land so I'll die to get that land. My country is God's favored nation on earth (that's what we all say), and I'm fighting God's battle if I lay down my life for my country."

For while we have plenty of patriotism within a given country, we seem to forget that because I love my country, somebody else must love his country. Because I love my garden and the hills across the valley, some other man loves his garden and the hills across his valley. And he loves his just as much as I love mine. Until the super-patriots of the earth learn that truth, we have little hope. The world is dying for want of a new patriotism, in which each of us will love the whole world as much as we love our own country; just as we have learned to love all America as we do the hills near home.

On a street car the other day I saw a sign which said, "Live and let live." I suppose that is a slogan for motorists, but it is a good slogan for statesmen and patriots too. Live and let live. I should like to write that on neon tubes and put that sign over the door of every council of war from Tokio, to Berlin, to Washington.

We use the same power of patriotism to put things together or to break them apart; it is just the way we handle that power that makes the difference.

But to turn for a moment from the more public phase of this theme to a realm much more personal, think of the electric power in this thing we call love to hold things together or break them apart. Who can fathom the mystery of the things we do for love, love of one kind or another? We laughingly say, "He's not responsible, he's in love." But that's not true. He is responsible—although he may not know it. He is responsible for what happens to him and to her and to them together. He is held quite definitely responsible for the consequences of his love, no matter how irresponsible it may seem. Here is the point, love of a man for a maid, or a maid for a man, can, at its best, take up a mediocre personality and give that personality radiance and purpose and health and joy unspeakable. Love like that at its best can hold a man together when he is in danger of going to pieces. It can set up a little family that will hold together for twenty, forty, maybe sixty years. Love like that holds the world together but you do not read about it in the papers, it is too quiet, too deep, too wonderful for words.

But let love at its worst go to it, and see what happens. It breaks up a man and makes him a beast. It torments a woman and drives her crazy. It tears families apart at Reno or some place nearer and less expensive. "We use the same power to put things together or to break them apart; it's just the way we handle that power that makes the difference."

And think, too, of the power of religion. The very word means "to bind together." That is what it should do for us. Make us whole. But when religion tears us apart, and sets us against each other, we have profaned it.

Power should be handled with care. It can put things together or it can break them apart.

JUST GENERAL DELAY

COMING back from Chicago not long ago the train was late. Turning to the porter I asked, "Porter, why is this train late?"

"Just general delay, sir, just general delay," was his laconic answer. No heavy snow had fallen, the passenger traffic was normal, the cold weather was not cold enough to make a great slowing of the steam pressure, but the train was late. Just general delay.

More than we ever guess, our lives are like that train, behind time when we ought to be on time. And if anybody has the nerve to ask us why we are late, the answer could be the same, just general delay.

So I am speaking to all of us today, poor humans who for no particular good reason fall behind schedule and come in late when we ought to be on time. How clearly we can classify most of our friends as people who are either on time or late for their daily appointments. In fact, there are a few people we can always count upon to be a little early. If the train leaves at noon they will be in the waiting room at 11:30 and they boast that they have not missed a train in fifty years. If church begins at eleven they are the kind of people who will be quietly meditating in the pew at quarter of eleven.

But most of us are in a wholly different category. We get up at the last moment and come downstairs while the breakfast bell is ringing its last warning. Or we race for the 8:15 commuter's train and catch the last step of the last car. And why are we late? No reason in particular, just general delay. But it would be almost as easy to be generally on time.

Now let it be said right here, that there are times when delay is the very essence of wisdom. When two young fools, a boy and a girl in their teens, meet each other on Saturday, fall in love at first sight and decide to elope on Monday, the thing they need most is a little delay. In fact a lot of delay is what their parents would pray for and what the police would enforce and what the parson should suggest. The old proverb, "Marry in haste and repent at leisure," is intended to show how high a premium ought to be put on delaying marriage long enough to be sure it will have half a chance of succeeding. But if there are some fools who get married too soon there are others, fools no less, who wait too long. Eager to provide a cushion for every possible emergency, waiting to solve every problem before they come to it, some of the saddest people we know are the people past their thirtieth year who could have arranged the wedding if they would but are guilty of just general delay. Thus they drift on into old age without making their dreams come true. More men than this world will ever know about have delayed their choice of a wife so long that they missed their first choice and sometimes their last choice.

There are girls who could not make up their minds, but life moved on and made their choice for them, and perhaps an unhappier choice than they might have made for themselves.

One thing you and I can be sure of in times like these is that there are countless questions up before us, personal and public questions, waiting for decision, and while we have all the time we need to make the right decision, we surely have no time to waste in delaying that decision. Carlyle put it clearly when he said, "It is one of the illusions, that the present hour is not the critical, decisive hour. Write it on your heart that every day is the best day in the year. No man has learned anything rightly until he knows and feels that every day is doomsday." Multitudes are in the valley of decision every day and almost every hour. Knowing when to delay and when to decide is about the most delicate kind of knowledge a man ever needs, but he needs it often and always.

One of the first places where delay is dangerous is in taking personal responsibility for our own conduct. All through childhood years we tend to stay tied to mother's apron strings and to put off the day when we stand on our own feet morally and make our own decisions. Even children of ten years of age ought to be making some of their own decisions, how they shall use their play time, what books they will enjoy reading, by what routine they will do the little chores assigned to them about the house. When a young man of twenty-four can say, as he did not long ago, "All my life my parents have made my decisions for me and now that I am away from home I find I cannot make wise decisions for myself," something is wrong, and that something is just general delay in that young man's taking control of his own life. I sometimes think our personal character is trained the way an airplane pilot learns to fly. The training plane has dual controls. The first flights find the student letting the teacher take control of the plane, while the student lets his hands be guided by the teacher's wisdom. After many hours of watching and testing and trials and an occasional turning of the control over to the student with the teacher ready to take over if the student misses the trick, there comes a great day when the teacher walks out to the plane with the student, but does not get in. "You can do it," he says, and pushes the student in with one word, "Solo." And the boy does it. He is in full control because he has learned from a good teacher how to take control. And if he has learned his lessons well he flies on his own and keeps his head above the ground and strikes a level course. Such is flying, and such is life.

In the early years, let a young man or woman take heed unto his ways, and study the way in which he shall go, keeping his eye on a good teacher, perchance his mother or father, possibly his school master, maybe a scout master, perchance the Man of Galilee. But when the fullness of the time comes, there is no general delay in taking over the controls and steering a steady course into the upper air, on high levels of thinking and acting. I wonder if any one of us has delayed too long in taking control of our own living, our own deciding, our own action. Delay is dangerous.

Another place where delay is dangerous is in checking on your physical condition. I am no doctor nor the son of a doctor but I see so much illness that could have been prevented that I make bold to step out of my supposed limits as a parson and ask you not to put off any longer that careful check-up of your body which is the temple of the Holy Spirit, if you have had no such check in the last three years. It may be that only a slight maladjustment needs to be set right for you to look better and feel better every day, so that you will be able to say with more than usual sincerity what Coué taught many people to repeat like parrots, "Every day in every way I'm growing better and better." It is common knowledge today how many serious diseases begin with slight symptoms that can be checked by skilled physicians but completely missed by amateurs. Often imperfect eyesight will cause excess fatigue and, remember, just general delay can be dangerous.

But if I say one word about the dangers of delaying the care of your body I want to say two words about the dangers of delaying the care of your mind.

What new skill have you learned in the last ten years? What new mental interest have you cultivated in the last five years? What books have you read and deeply enjoyed in the last year? What lectures have you heard and then followed up on your own initiative? Nowhere is delay more dangerous than in neglecting to feed the gray matter in your skull with sound food. You would not think of missing your dinner one day in three hundred sixty-five, but millions of us go not only for days but sometimes for years, without feeding the brain a single bite of strong food that will take chewing to digest. And why? Just general delay.

With libraries and art museums and natural history collections there is no excuse for the way our minds get behind the times through general delay.

But if we are guilty of general delay in our personal choices, the same trouble holds true in many larger spheres of public debate and policy. Elijah condemned the people with, "How long halt ye between two opinions? If the Lord be God, follow him, but if Baal, then follow him."

How well we know the sickness of Hamlet when, "The native hue of resolution is sicklied o'er with the pale cast of thought, and enterprises of great pith and moment lose the name of action."

For one thing look at what delay has cost the Christian Church, our delay in making the world into the Kingdom of God instead of into the Kingdom of the Caesars and the Charlemagnes and the Rasputins and the Hitlers. For two thousand years the Church has been trying to bring the Kingdom of God to earth and in many ways we are farther away from it than ever before. I say we supposed Christians, with great cathedrals towering to the sky in almost every city of the world, with big and little churches in almost every crossroads town of the western world, what have we done with our power and our money and our time and our people? We have brought the world to the edge of another primeval jungle. I say shame upon us, one by one and all together, that we could not have done better while it was not too late, and I trust it is not too late now to save the world from bleeding itself to death in colossal suicide. My humble belief is this, the Church has been guilty of just general delay, it has lived in the past instead of the future, it has taken the world as it was and not as it has come to be. We have been reminiscent instead of prophetic. And this general delay will cost us a terrible penny, not a pretty one, before we get this world back on its way to the Kingdom of God instead of the Kingdom of Hell.

Well, it may be later than we think, but it is not too late, personally or publicly. There is no personal fault which we cannot begin to set right beginning now. There is no public wrong so tragic but that together we can start to change that wrong into right. No situation is ever hopeless, even in a time of general delay.

FREE AS THE AIR?

EVERYBODY likes a bargain. Let it be noised about that something is being given away free and a crowd gathers in a hurry. The question I ask today is this: are these give-aways as free as they seem? Does not somebody always have to pay for what we may get freely? Or perchance do we not ourselves pay in other coin than we expected?

Not long ago a man with a big box stood near the curb, ostensibly giving something away. As I drove by he waved a small carton toward me as much as to say, "Here's a free sample, take it with you." Well, I am human, glad to have a free present any time. So I stopped, opened the car window, and reached for the free sample. The man at the curb tossed the carton in to me and said. "Here are some free soap flakes for your wife." I shouted my thanks and started to drive off, but he kept the door open and added, "Say, mister, you shave, don't you?" That question showed remarkable insight. "Now here is another package of fine shaving soap. If you'll buy this shaving soap I'll give you the soap chips for your wife." "But," I protested, "I thought you were giving away the soap chips." "Sure, I am, if you buy the shaving soap."

I weakened a little and asked, "How much is the

shaving soap?" "Only seventy-five cents." "No, I don't need any shaving soap." "But, wait, I'll give you three boxes of soap flakes free if you'll buy just one box of shaving soap."

By that time I had finally discovered what I should have guessed in the first place. He was not giving anything away. You paid for those soap flakes and you paid dearly.

Most things in this world that have a label on them, "Free," have a hidden price tag, somewhere.

Take the freest thing on earth, the air we breathe. It may be free to us but it costs God something to make it. Somewhere a great mind, the mind of God, evolved a mixture of ozone and oxygen and nitrogen, in just the right proportions to make air that is good to breathe.

Or sunlight. We take that freely enough, but who can estimate its cost to the Creator who maintains the sun in its unwearied course, age after age, undiminished in its burning power, seemingly supplied with an inexhaustible supply of fuel. Sunlight is free to us but it is not free to God. Somebody, somewhere, has to create it if we are to enjoy it.

Or take water, is that free? Not that I know of. If you live on a farm you at least have to pump it up out of the well, you pay that much for your water anyway. And those of us who live in the cities and pay water bills know by a pretty penny a year that water is not free. Not long ago the Governor opened the valves to let water from Quabbin Reservoir pour into Boston to quench our parched throats. Is that water free? Not by the $27,000,000 it took to build it. Not by the six towns that had to move out of the valley or be inundated. Not by the sixty miles of piping that had to be laid into the city. Water is not free and never will be. You either have to kneel down to its level to drink it or pump it up to your level to pour it between your lips.

Perhaps in your town you have what is called a "Free Library." It may be free to you but it cost plenty to build it. In hundreds of towns in the West I have seen Carnegie Free Libraries. Not only Andrew Carnegie, but the men who sweated for him, helped to build those libraries. And somebody cut the stone and planned the archway and chose the books. And when you go into a Free Library you must have paid the cost of learning how to read if you are to enjoy that Free Library. There is no such thing, literally, as a Free Library. Libraries are built at great cost, and they are enjoyed by people whose reading habits are learned at great cost of personal discipline.

So you can listen to free music on your radio, but remember the cost of producing that music, the hours of rehearsal, the years of study prerequisite to the mastery of the flute or the bass viol or the French horn. And when we listen to music we must bring to it a soul big enough to appreciate the finest or we shall call the finest symphony, "Horsehair scraping on cat-gut." Great music costs something to make and it costs something to enjoy.

So we speak of a Free Museum of Art. But the pictures were not painted freely. They cost keen study of line and color and perspective, years of apprenticeship in the fine arts. Every good picture costs the artist far more than he ever gets paid for it. And when you go to the museum to enjoy fine art you must pay the first price of taking the trouble to go. For mark this, although a museum may be free, thousands of people have never been through its doors because they are not interested in that sort of thing. Free, it costs too much trouble to go. And after getting inside you will say, "What is it all about?" unless you take with you a hunger for beauty and a thirst for artistic meaning and a longing for good color and the comedy and tragedy of life. Art is never free.

Move now into the realm of free government. How much we cherish what we call free democracy and how often we forget its high cost. We take free democracy for granted, think we shall always have it, just because we have it now. That is the quickest way to lose it. Free government costs the careful vote of every citizen. Free government asks the citizen to pay taxes to protect his home from fire and to educate his children. In a truer sense, then, there is no such thing as free government. There is only government at terribly high cost.

How often we talk about personal freedom, the right to do what we want to do when we want to do it. Epictetus gave us the truth about that kind of freedom when he said, "No man is free who is not master of himself." So even personal freedom comes at a high price, only when a man has tempered his passions with reason, his beastly instincts with human affection and moral judgment and has become free to do what he knows he ought to do, rather than just what he wants to do.

Yet another phrase that is often bandied about is free love. That means making love without taking the responsibilities of love. Love one woman for a season and then try another. That is the way love goes on in the jungle. But among human beings it is not as free as it sounds. For love like that pays a terribly high price. It gives up the lifetime devotion of one man for one woman, on all levels of companionship, mental and spiritual as well as physical. Free love, here today and gone tomorrow, knows nothing about loyalty and sacrifice for each other and forgiveness and understanding and sharing sorrows together. Free love breaks two people apart as soon as the going gets hard and makes them fend for themselves, alone. And what does free love know about standing by the children of that love through the years when children need a father and a mother more than they need bread and butter? Free love is not free, therefore. It costs infinitely more than it is worth. As Lowell put it,

> Baubles we buy with a whole soul's taking.
> 'Tis only God can be had for the asking.

But even God is not entirely free. Our souls must

long for Him before we find Him. Our hearts must
be restless before we find our rest in Him. Follow
Augustine through his confessions and see the high
price he paid to find God. Look at Jesus in Geth-
semane and on Calvary and you will see that God did
not come easily to Jesus. We are bought with a price.
God pays part of that price, Jesus pays what he can in
showing us the way to God, but part of the price is
left in our account and in our name. Unless we pay
that price we never come close to God.

That is why it is a mistake to talk too much about a
free church. Every church ever built was raised, from
its foundation up, by the high cost of people who
cared enough to pay that cost.

Even salvation is not free in that it takes no effort
from us. The other day a young man went to his minister and said he had just been converted, but would
the minister please pay his debts at the liquor store
and the clothing house, totalling forty-eight dollars.
Should that minister pay that young man's debts?
That would indeed be free salvation.

No, sir. When a man comes to God, wakes up to
the purpose for which he was born, turns about and
starts toward heaven instead of toward hell, he knows
the high cost of what he has done, if he knows anything at all. He pays his own debts as soon as he can,
both money debts and moral debts. He sets straight
every crooked place that he had made crooked, so far
as he is able. He makes amends for his mistakes and
tries to mend the broken hearts. Free religion? Free

salvation? The only kind I know anything about is expensive religion, high cost salvation.

It is an old saying that "the best things in life are free." I am not so sure. Perhaps the best things in life are expensive. Free education is free only to begin with. Then it takes the student's hard work, his creative imagination to search out the answers to hard questions. The other day, at Tufts College I saw the majority of students playing on the grassy fields—football, golf, tennis, track. But off in a corner of the campus I watched a handful of students working hard with pick and shovel, leveling off a rocky terrain. My professor friend told us that in that pick and shovel gang were three of his best students. They had to work their way through college. But when they finished work and started to study they knew what they wanted and they got their dollar's worth of tuition because they had earned the dollar in the first place. So I am sure that our best students all over America today are not the ones who take their education as a free gift, handed to them on a silver platter. The future leaders of America are the students who know the high cost of education, because they are paying that cost in blisters on their hands, nights spent washing dishes in restaurants, shovelling coal into somebody's furnace. Free education? Expensive education is nearer the truth.

The next time you hear somebody talking about how free America is, you remind them of how expensive America is, if we are to keep her free.

LO, THE POOR INDIAN

Lo, the poor Indian, whose untutored mind
Sees God in clouds, or hears him in the wind;
His soul proud Science never taught to stray
Far as the solar walk or milky way.
                    —ALEXANDER POPE.

ONCE every year, on April 19th, a half million people stand in the rain or roast in the sun to watch the most famous sporting event in New England, the Boston Marathon.

A full-blooded Narragansett Indian held the record for this twenty-five-mile, man-killing endurance test, a record he won in 1939.

I am glad to see an Indian win something because, since Kit Carson and General Custer, the Indians have been losing a great deal, by the trickery of their "white brothers."

In the folklore of the Iroquois tribe, near old Buffalo on the Niagara River, it was an axiom, that if an Indian dreamt that something happened to him, that dream must come true, by fair means or foul. One Iroquois, Chief Henry, happened to be at the trading post when the trader opened a box of handsome uniforms for the resident soldiers, adorned with gold braid and shiny buttons. The chief came in the next day to say, "I dreamt that you gave me one of those uniforms." The trader handed it over, knowing that if he refused that Indian would be his enemy for life. But the trader was not outwitted. The following day he met Chief Henry and surprised him with, "Chief, I dreamt that you gave me that five hundred acres of land your tribe owns beyond the bend in the Creek." "All right," answered the chief, "you can have it, but I won't dream with you any more."

That is a fair sample of the kind of tricks we have been playing on the Indians for a long time now. So is it any wonder that the red men have had to be crafty themselves to salvage even a trace of what was originally all theirs?

Living in the forest, untainted by the sins of white men, the Indian was never so poor and depraved a savage as he sometimes appears now that civilization has spoiled his natural habitat and habits.

Who taught the Indian, with fiendish persistence, the excessive use of firewater and firearms, the two devilish damnations which the Indian could not handle with any common sense because he was so naïve and forest-born?

Red Jacket, the wise orator of the Iroquois, speaking to his white brothers in Buffalo, said several things rather plainly:

"You have taken a number of our young men to your schools. You have educated them and taught

them your religion. They have returned to their
kindred and color, neither white men nor Indians.
The arts they have learned are incompatible with
the chase and ill adapted to our customs. They have
been taught that which is useless to us. They have
been made to feel artificial wants, which never entered the minds of their brothers. They have imbibed, in your great towns, the seeds of vices which
were unknown in the forest. They become discour-
aged and dissipated, despised by the Indians, neglected by the whites and without value to either."

Of course the missionaries explained with great
care the life and crucifixion of Jesus, whereupon Red
Jacket answered, "You say that you destroyed the
Son of the Great Spirit. Perhaps this is the merited
cause of all your troubles and misfortunes. But,
brother, bear in mind that we had no participation
in this murder. We disclaim it; we love the Great
Spirit. And as we never had any part in so unjust,
so merciless an outrage, the Great Spirit therefore
continues to smile upon us and to give us, in our
natural state, peace, joy and plenty."

As a fair test of the quality of the religion of the
white men, Red Jacket made this suggestion, "Go,
then, and teach the whites. Select, for example, the
people of Buffalo. We will be spectators, and remain
silent. Improve their morals and refine their habits.
Make them less disposed to cheat the Indians, to make
them drunk and to take from them their lands. Let us
know the tree by the blossoms, and the blossoms by

the fruit. When this shall be made clear to our minds we may be more willing to listen to you. But until then we must be allowed to follow the religion of our ancestors."

As early as 1609 Champlain had taught the Indians near the site of Ticonderoga the fatal power of gunpowder. And in that same year, it is possible that Henry Hudson, moving up the river which now bears his name, in the *Half Moon,* first taught the Indians the use of firewater. Tradition describes that first sad lesson, when the Indians thought that Hudson, in his red cloak, must be Manito, the Great Spirit, coming to them for a visit. As he came ashore, the Indians gathered about in reverent respect. "The Manito had a little cup which was transparent. From a bockhack he poured a liquid into the cup, drank it, poured more, offered it to the chief, who smelled it, passed it to his brothers. But Manito seemed angry that they did not drink, so the chief quaffed the cup to its bottom. There was no sudden change in his actions, though the Indians may have feared poison, but ere long his limbs relaxed. His eyes closed lustreless, and he rolled heavy and helpless upon the ground. His friends supposed him dead. After a long time their chief began to revive. He rose upon his feet joyously, declared that he had experienced the most delightful sensations while in the trance. He had seen visions. He requested another draught and the liquor was poured out for them all. They all partook of the ravishing cup and all became intoxicated."

That was the start of a bitter end for Indians who could never learn to drink with moderation. In 1721 Charlevoix writes, "Those who have greatest reason to reproach themselves with the horrors of Indian intoxication are the ones to ask whether they are Christians. But can those who, in cold blood, and with a perfect knowledge of what they are about, reduce these simple people to this condition, from sordid motives of avarice, can they be imagined to have any religion at all? An Indian will give all he is worth for one glass of brandy. This is strong temptation to dealers, against which neither the exclamations of their pastors, nor the zeal and authority of the magistrate, nor respect for the laws, nor the dread of the judgments of the Almighty, nor the thoughts of a hell hereafter, of which these barbarians exhibit a very striking picture, have been able to avail."

From start to finish, our endeavors to change the pattern of the Indian's life to match our own highly complex civilization, have met with failure. Even the wise and good things we have suggested have not always met with success. Colonel Roosevelt visited Chief Parker in Oklahoma and said, "Chief, you live like a white man almost every way, but you have five wives and you should have only one. Now you ought to give up four of your wives." The chief answered, "You are my great white father, and I will do as you wish, on one condition. You pick out the one I am to live with and then you go tell the other four."

The thing I admire about the Indian who held the

marathon record is his endurance, his power to stay with a race for twenty-five miles. That is the kind of thing all of us need, for we live in a day which puts a gaudy premium on high speed for the short run instead of endurance for the long haul. In an older generation the One Hoss Shay was built in such a logical way that it ran a hundred years to a day. But now a car is out of style in one year and out of the running in three years, on the average.

This passion for temporariness instead of permanence has gotten over into character, too, where, as Arnold Bennett says about novel writing, "Anybody can write a good first chapter."

Look around you in school and watch the students who write a good first chapter. They start with a sprint that dazzles even the teacher but on the first long hill they fade back, get careless with the homework, get tired of the daily discipline. They never find their second wind.

Look around you in business and listen to the men who have ideas that never get beyond the castle-in-the-air stage. They write a good first chapter but the middle of the book is blank.

Look around you on Beacon Street or Shady Lane and see the couples who wrote a good first chapter in marriage. It began with, "I think you're wonderful," then came dishes and bills and babies and arguments and the middle chapters are not so romantic as the first. It takes endurance. Marriage is meant to be a marathon, not a sprint.

Look around you in church and see the people who began with enthusiasm the life of religion. Now they have grown cold and formal and wholly lack-lustre. Their religion looks like a burden instead of a dynamic, radiant power. They wrote a good first chapter, but. Endurance is still one of the greatest things in the world, especially when it is built into a human personality.

I remember another Indian who had endurance. He was a medicine man among the Navajos and I met him as we camped in the shadow of Rainbow Bridge in Southern Utah. In his deep voice he asked for a cup of coffee and, while he sipped it, I asked him some questions.

"Does your kind of medicine always make people well?"

"No," he confessed, "me medicine sometimes good, sometimes bad."

"When is it bad?" I probed.

"When me squaw, she ver' sick, me medicine no good, me take squaw to white man doctor."

"But how did you carry her to white man doctor?"

"Me put squaw on pinto pony in front, then me ride behind."

"Where did you find white man doctor in this wild desert?"

"Oljato, white man doctor there."

I had heard of Oljato but I knew it was many miles distant from Rainbow Bridge, so I asked, "How far is it to Oljato from here? How far did you take your squaw to white man doctor?"

"Me no savez, me jus' go," was his short answer, the best sermon in as few words as I have ever heard. He did not know how far it was, his squaw was sick, so he just went.

I have seen Indians living in the Painted Desert Navajo and Hopi reservations where they have to plant corn in hills nine feet apart to get any kind of crop at all, yet somehow they live. And somehow they keep happy. I have heard their primitive songs, coming in plaintive melody over the echoing canyons by bright starlight. I have seen them in ceremonial dances which seem to recreate for them the glory and the majesty of other days.

Lo, the poor Indian!

ALONE AND TOGETHER

> Though we are comrades and eagerly try
> To approach each other,
> There are spaces not to be crossed,
> And we wander alone.

FROM my window on Beacon Street I see a man. He walks with straight precision; his hair is gray about the temples; his skin is well tanned by wind and sun; when he turns this way I can see that he is very much on the handsome side. Usually an eager dog strains at the leash as he strolls across Beacon Street or down the Esplanade or across Boston Common. Often he walks alone. He is the only man in history who has explored both the North and South Poles. He has flown the North Atlantic when it was more of an adventure than it is now. His name is Richard E. Byrd.

And for a man so heavy with honors, he carries them lightly and humbly. For a man of action he is an uncommonly good writer, with a prose style full of careful description and poetic insight and clarity.

His best book is called *Alone* and it is the story of five months spent almost in the shadow of the South Pole in a tiny hut, during the Antarctic winter of

1934. When that hut of flimsy boards was put on exhibition in the Boston Public Library, cues of vicarious thrill seekers, a quarter mile long, waited hours to step near the little stove which had almost killed Byrd with its fumes.

Why does he so capture our imaginations? Because he dared to live alone. He was thrown back upon his own inner resources of mind and body and spirit. Drifting snow covered his little house so that his only exit was a hole in the roof. The small stove gave his only heat to fight the cold which often fell to 60° below zero. When fumes almost killed him he had to put out the fire and freeze, rather than suffocate. So for half of each day he kept the fire going. For the rest of the day he smothered the fire and nearly froze. But I should not say "day" because he lived in perpetual night for all five months of that Antarctic winter. His only light was the flashing glory of the *aurora australis,* arching the sky over his head with flaming gold and orange and steely blue.

People still ask why on earth Byrd chose to isolate himself in such complete solitude. Let him answer our wondering in his own words, "I wanted to sink roots into some replenishing philosophy. I wanted time to read, to study, to think, to listen to the phonograph. I wanted to be able to live exactly as I chose, obedient to no necessities but those imposed by wind and night and cold, and to no man's laws but my own. That was the way I saw it," says Byrd. Beyond these personal reasons there was also Byrd's

desire to examine the weather conditions at the South
Pole which are now known to affect the weather of
the whole world.

Many people in this world would like to be alone
once in a while, but they never can, because they
cannot escape family or friends or enemies on the
right hand and on the left. And just as sad are the
people who would like to be together with other
people but cannot because they seem doomed to
loneliness—no friends, no work, no hobbies, no family. If it is bad business never to be alone, it is just
as bad business always to be alone.

Now taking modern life for what it is for most of
us—an inevitable rubbing of elbows with other people in subway cars, at the time clock or even in
church—what chance has anybody to be alone? Just
this, each one of us is alone in a crisis. We have to
make our own decisions when those decisions are
most important. It is alone that most of us must face
temptation and sorrow. Just as Jesus went into the
wilderness alone, to face the temptings of the devil,
and just as Jesus went into the Garden of Geth-
semane to face his sorrow, alone, so you and I come to
these two battlefields, alone. Now do not misunderstand me, our religion and our friends and our education can help us prepare to meet temptation, but
when a man comes to a crossroad and one voice says,
"Here, take it easy and don't be too particular about
your conduct," and another voice says, "Be a man,
not a coward," the decision is made alone. Our

guardians cannot follow us around every corner to see that we do not trip. We have to pick up our own feet. The kind of person I become is decided by the kind of decisions I make—alone. And too many of us flounder in the valleys of indecision because we are waiting for somebody else to make up our minds for us, when we ought to do it *alone,* and do it quickly. To drink or not to drink? Get all the evidence you can, see what happens to other people, then decide for yourself, alone. To be honest or to cut the corners? Get all the advice from all the advisers you wish, read books on the subject, then decide, alone. To walk the high road of moral integrity or to slip into the slime of lust? Look around you and see what that choice, either way, has done to the people you know and love and admire or to the ones you despise. Then make your own decision, alone, and be sure not to let anybody else make it for you. For the world is full of wrecked lives, cast up on a rocky shore because the captain was asleep in his cabin, letting some other navigator make his decisions for him. Note that when Jesus faced the devil in the wilderness alone, he told that devil where to go, and he told him, alone. "Get thee behind me, Satan."

So it is with the sorrows that come to everyone sooner or later. You will find comfort in what your friends say and do for you. Great books, especially the Bible, and great poetry, will lend a helping hand. But at long last you will have to conquer that sorrow alone, or it will never be conquered.

But if we have to face our crises alone, let it be said quickly that we face the common round of living *together,* not alone. Nobody but a hermit can live alone, and that is not very good for him. Be alone once in a long while, but be able to live with other people most of the time—that is the only way you can live, happily.

Children grow up healthy-minded only when they grow up together. A child forced to eat alone, play alone, talk only to himself is a problem child right from the start. His only salvation is to have to think of other children, to understand them, to learn to be happy with them. Children have to live together. The happiest, most normal homes I know are those where young people are always bringing their friends home to meet mother and father. That is right, because they are living together.

And what is marriage when it is right, unless it is what one poet has called, "The Dear Togetherness"?

And yet even the well-married need times of being alone. Gibran suggests this necessity in his lines,

You were born together, and together you shall be forevermore.
But let there be spaces in your togetherness,
And let the winds of the heavens dance between you.
Love one another, but make not a bond of love:
Let it rather be a moving sea between the shores of your souls.
Fill each other's cup but drink not from one cup.

Give one another of your bread but eat not from the same
loaf.

Sing and dance together and be joyous, but let each one
of you be alone.

Even as the strings of a lute are alone though they quiver
with the same music.

Give your hearts, but not into each other's keeping.

For only the hand of life can contain your hearts.[1]

So there is a time to be alone. That is the time of
inner crisis.

And there is a time to be together. And that is
every day's common living.

[1] From "The Prophet" by Kahlil Gibran. Reprinted by permission of Alfred Knopf Company.

PIN POINTS

I HAVE been challenged to use a common pin for a text. I accept. The first thing I notice about a pin is that it has one good point.

A pin without one good point is like a cart without wheels or a boat without a rudder—it misses the point of its existence.

Now, not only is a pin pointless without one good point, so is a human being. God created us as free men and women whose lives are supposed to come to a clear-cut point somewhere. Our education, our experience of days and years is meant to sharpen that point so that we come to a focus upon some problem of living and penetrate that problem by the sharpness of our action.

No life is mature until it comes to a point somewhere, focuses with sharp detail on some vocation or avocation and ceases to be so eternally and infernally well rounded that it has no good point. For here is one of the subtlest dangers of our modern living—that with morning and evening newspapers each as big as a book, with endless radio programs to listen to most of the day and night, with cars to ride and pictures to see our lives become diffuse and blunted until we lose all possible point of influence. We are jacks of all trades and masters of none. Whether we like it or not we live in a world where lives that do not develop a sharp point somewhere are doomed to disappointment.

Now, mark you, I am not pleading for specialization that rules out all the normal well-rounded fullness of life. Let every man be a good family man, that is a man's happiest business. Let every man be a good friend, a good lover, a good husband, a good father, those are the highest vocations on earth. Let every woman know how to boil water and bake a cake and live within her budget, almost. That has been nearly every woman's business since Eve. All of us ought to know how to get along with people. That is the elementary business of living. But over and beyond all that, we owe it to ourselves and to the God who gave us life to sharpen our wits in one of the arts or crafts so that we may create something plus, over and beyond the elementals. So, if you spend every spare moment you can garner from the grim business of living to play the Moonlight Sonata on your cheap violin, but you keep at it until you play that Moonlight Sonata to your own deep happiness, your life has come to a point, a good point. If you steal away on a Saturday afternoon with your oils and easel and take your stance near a wooden bridge and then focus your eye and soul on perspective and color and line, your life has come to a point, a good point. If you cherish great books because they lead you to writing your own thoughts, your life has come to a point. If your daily work has so captured your imagination that the days are not half long enough to carry out the dreams of what you would like to create, your life has come to a point.

On the other hand, if your hours hang heavy on your hands, and the days drag on into weeks of boredom and there is little or nothing you get excited about, then you might as well attend your own funeral, for your life has indeed come upon tragedy—it has lost its point.

The second thing I notice about a common pin is that it goes straight to the point. A crooked pin is not much use, neither is a crooked man. But the woods are full of crooked men, and the cities too. They may not be badly crooked, most of them, just a little bent. You may not notice it even, but a close examination of their lives by their wives, or by God, or by themselves, would reveal that they are not quite straight. Each one of us knows what this means. We do not have to think long to discover some little or big area of our conduct where we are not as straight as we know we ought to be. A little crookedness has crept in and we are hesitant to straighten it out. But sometimes things need straightening out.

The season of the year just before Christmas is Advent, a time of preparation for the coming of Jesus. The call of John the Baptist was this, "Prepare ye the way of the Lord, and the crooked shall be made straight." That is not a bad kind of preparation for Christmas, making some of the crooked places straight and—let each of us say—beginning with me. So often we are experts at straightening other people's business while we do nothing about the crookedness in our own. Perhaps before Christmas, some of us will have to straighten out a crooked business deal that is not fair; not by any honorable standard could that deal stand the light of day. Straighten it out if it is crooked. Some of us will have to straighten out the crooked place at home where love that ought to be straight as a pin is all twisted into crookedness that will not stand up under our own conscience. Some of us will have to straighten out friendships that have been badly bent on the rocks of selfishness and gossip and misunderstanding. Just before Christmas is a good time to be as good as we can be, and straighten out the crooked places. Crooked politics and crooked diplomacy are somebody's business and this world would be spared a mountain of poverty and tears and bloodshed if we could have a Christmas Truce and straighten out some of the crookedness that goes on behind the political scenes all the way from Boston to Moscow. A pin goes straight to the point. So should a human soul.

The next interesting thing about a common pin is that it keeps its head. A pin without a head is almost no use at all. Neither is a man. And when a man really uses his head great things begin to happen. Of late, intellectual activity has been rather disparaged. We say in ridicule, "He's all brains and no heart." We never like a man to be so wound up in mental cogitations that he cannot let his life be moved by affection and emotion and pathos. But is it any more of a compliment to say of a man, "He is all heart and no brains"? Or is it really a compliment to say of a woman, "She's a beauty, but no brains"? Whether we openly admit it or not, we like a woman with intellectual stability, brains back of her beauty, else her beauty may get both her and us into endless trouble. Let it be said for America's sanity at this present moment, that the most popular women in the country, even by vote of the college boys, are the women, like Dorothy Thompson, who are marked for their brains, whatever other charms they may have incidentally.

Dr. Fosdick points out in one of his great sermons that most of the mistakes in this world are not the result of deliberate wrongdoing, but of stupidity. Jesus was crucified by stupidity, "They knew not what they did." Nobody sets out to be bad purposely, intentionally. Somebody makes a bad judgment, does something stupid, and that stupidity leads to more and more mistakes and, in the end, those almost unintentional mistakes lead to a tragic consequence called sin, or war, or loneliness, or remorse. Yea, Lord, deliver us from our sins, but deliver us also from our lack of intelligence, our lack of brains, our unwillingness to use the brains Thou gavest us. Forgive us our propensity for acting on hot, fevered impulse and emotion rather than on considered judgments, thought through to their consequences in us and in those we love and in the world around us.

The last important fact about a common pin is that its purpose in life is to hold things together. And that is a purpose than which there is no other more admirable.

In a world that is falling apart, cut asunder by hatred and war, bleeding and broken, how we need a mighty pin to hold that world together, and if we cannot find a safety pin, why can we not find a common pin, or an uncommon pin, anything, to hold the world together? I know what would do it—kindness, love, religion. But try to find them and try to fasten them to the broken parts of the earth. The very word "religion" comes from the Latin, *religare*, which means to bind together. So religion has the same purpose as a common pin, and that is a high calling—to hold things together.

Or when a man is in danger of going to pieces morally, think what it means if religion, like a pin, can hold him together, keep him from breaking up. And what shall we say of a home where soon, unless something wonderful happens, that family will break up and go to pieces? Where is a pin to hold that family together? I will tell you where. Simple, genuine, clear religion will do it, if it gets a chance. Love will do it, love that deepens and heightens with the years and knows how to forgive and how to rebuild.

More than anything else today we stand in need of spiritual pins to hold life together and keep it from breaking up into pieces that all the king's horses and all the king's men could never put together again.

A common pin has one good point.

A common pin comes straight to the point.

A common pin has a good head.

A common pin holds things together.

INSURANCE

From my windows on life, in what should have been the deadly stillness of the after-midnight hours, there arose such a clatter I went to the window to see what was the matter. Students in their pajamas were piling into their ramshackle jallopies and shouting, "Hurry up, Tom, the fire will be out before you get there."

A little too sleepy and a little too old to chase the fire engines as I used to, I ensconced myself in an arm chair near a window looking out over the Charles River to Cambridge and I enjoyed that rip-roaring blaze to the uttermost. A huge garage and storehouse with twenty-five trucks and tons of merchandise went up in smoke within a few minutes. As each gasoline tank blew up, sparks and flames curled skyward with a billowing heave. Fortunately it was a calm night, and the flames were mirrored in the river with almost perfect imagery. Cars streamed across the Harvard Bridge, late-stayers-up getting a last thrill before tumbling into bed. Sixteen blasts from the Cambridge fire whistle meant more help needed, or under control, I am not sure which.

At last all the gasoline had exploded, the roof had

fallen in, the inferno calmed down, and I went back
to bed, dreaming about the fires of other days that
live with such vivid crimson colors in my memory.
There must be many of you to whom fire has indeed
been your worst enemy, for it has done terrible
things to you or to those you loved and have lost a
while. For the rest of us fires are more an exciting
interlude in the midst of otherwise quiet and serene
days, and we enjoy them while we may.

I suppose we ought to thank whoever invented
fire insurance for taking some of the terror out of
the siren and the clanging bell. And today we can
buy insurance for almost every risk imaginable. Not
only life insurance and fire insurance and illness insurance, but not long ago an agent suggested that
I needed insurance for seven other possibilities. "You
should have lightning insurance, and windstorm, and
suppose hail breaks your windows? Then you ought
to have explosion insurance. And what if a riot
breaks in your door, do you have protection against
that? Then an automobile gone haywire may crash
into your house, do you have insurance against that?
And suppose an airplane falls out of the sky on your
roof, you ought to have insurance to cover that possibility."

Probably, as is said of Lloyd's in London, you can
buy insurance to protect yourself against loss from
almost any cause in earth or sky or under the earth.

One of the chief tendencies of our civilized life

today is to try to cushion ourselves against every emergency or accident. We call it social security, and everybody wants it. We want to be insured somehow against the loss of our jobs, against the losses brought about by illness, against fire and flood and death. Now with this trend of civilization toward trying to cushion every bump I am in full accord, especially for the people who get more than their share of bumps.

There is at least one thing in this world that I would put above security, however, as the goal of life, that one thing is courage. We give our deepest admiration, not to the people whose motto is Safety First, but to those whose motto is "Truth First," and safety last. "Safety First" was not the motto of Jesus. He took very poor care of himself, crucified at thirty-three, but he took great care of other people's souls and bodies. Safety first was not the motto of Columbus, crossing an uncharted sea. Safety first was not the slogan of Lindbergh, over the Atlantic, or of Father Damien let loose among the lepers of the South Seas. While safety first is important anywhere, and especially in a factory where dangerous machinery is whirling through the air, safety first, as a philosophy of life has its limitations. It makes a man think of cushions rather than hard work. Not long ago I saw a laundry truck with a sign on the side, "Are you pillow conscious? Have your pillows renovated." Well, that is the danger of perfect security carried *ad nauseam,* it makes man who ought to be danger conscious, pillow conscious.

This pillow consciousness is like a line of an old hymn which is a little misleading. We often sing, "Hide me, O my Saviour, hide, till the storms of life be past." That is one prayer, but here is another prayer, "Lead me, O my Saviour, lead, through the storms of life."

Let us never forget that some kinds of insurance cannot be bought so surely as they can be attained by our own will and purpose and discipline.

Take sickness insurance. You can buy that at so much a year. But there is a better kind of sickness insurance that you can sell yourself. It is a long tramp this afternoon, an overnight trip to the mountains, a better night's sleep than you had last night.

Or what insurance is there that I will get a job after graduation next June? Or keep the job I have through the next layoff? There is no positive insurance for such a risk, but there is a kind of insurance likely to do the trick. That is the policy of doing some one job so well and knowing so much about it that you cannot help but become indispensable somewhere along the line. It is happening every day. Here is a little lunchroom that nobody thought could pay for itself. A young man and his wife took it over three months ago. They got up early and they stayed up late making the place attractive, learning to prepare good food at the lowest possible cost. Today they are doing better than anybody thought could be done. Their insurance was their own will and purpose and hard work.

Insure yourself against every possible emergency, as much by what you are as by what you pay in cash premiums.

IT'S LOVE THAT MAKES THE WORLD GO ROUND

It SEEMS to me very important that in a world like this, so hard driven by the necessities of tragedy, the finer feelings of romantic sentiment should be kept very much alive. One shudders to think of poor Dan Cupid trying to fly about in a stratosphere filled with bombing planes. His quiver full of arrows seems out of time and place. But even so, let's give Dan Cupid his due for it's love that makes the world go round.

Not the world of substance, eight thousand miles in diameter and twenty-five thousand miles in circumference, of course. That world goes round on the power of a cosmic momentum that no human mind can fathom. But I am speaking today of the world of human events, the world of activity around each of us as persons; it is these worlds that love makes go round.

Goethe puts the same idea in more classic language when he says, "We are shaped and fashioned by what we love." So, it's love of something or someone that makes our personal world go round. What we admire determines what we become, what we work for, what we live for, what we are.

First, let us take this phrase, "It's love that makes the world go round," in its most obvious meaning, the love of a man for a maid and a maid for a man. You all know a boy about twenty-two who was getting nowhere fast just a few months ago. Just out of school he had not found himself vocationally, he seemed lost in the wide, wide world. Then something happened to that boy now become a man. Cupid aimed an arrow straight for his heart and did not miss. He fell in love, completely, ecstatically, gloriously. Suddenly all the hidden powers in that man came to life. His homely face now seems rather handsome because he is in love. Although at first he showed symptoms of lovesickness he snapped out of that foolishness in a hurry because he had to settle down to hard work to buy that diamond and begin saving up for the little house or apartment. It's love that makes his world go round. Nothing else matters so much as that. All he does moves around that one focus, his love for the girl of his dreams.

And how shall I, a man, say what love means to the girl in the case? Byron said it first, and much better than I can: "Man's love is of man's life a part; 'tis woman's whole existence." So she, too, awakes from sleeping, and the world takes on new colors, new joys unspeakable and full of glory. It's love that makes her world go round. Make no mistake about that.

Long years after the wedding bells have echoed down into history, what brings him home out of the busy world on the 5:15 to clean the cellar, or cut the grass, or spade the garden or play tennis with the children? What keeps her at the ironing board and over the stove for thirty years? The cynic says it is just habit, forced routine, unimaginative repetition. Don't you believe it. Wherever that home is worth coming home to, it is love that makes that world go round, love grown rich and deep in its ample folds, love that nobody can understand who has not known it for the power that it is. In your homes you look at each other across the table, father to mother, children to parents, and you know what I'm talking about; it's love that makes the world go round.

But there are other kinds of love besides romantic love that make the world go round, sometimes in dizzy circles.

Look if you will, at the love of power that is sweeping the world off its feet. That makes the world go round, backwards, counter-clockwise, instead of forward. Here we thought we had delivered the earth forever from the tragic love of power vested in the mind of a Pharaoh or a Caesar or a Napoleon or a Kaiser, only to have this same inordinate love of power spring up to plague us in the twentieth century.

"Power politics," how that phrase describes the diplomacy of today. One little man wants power over his party in Germany. He gets it. Then he seeks power over a great nation and by hook or crook, he gets it. Then he seeks power over other smaller countries and by brute force he gets it. Power to get more power. I say it is this love of power that is making the world go round backwards, reeling and dizzy in the head.

Our only hope is the comforting epigram of Demosthenes, "It is not possible to found a lasting power upon injustice, perjury, and treachery." How we must believe that to be true. No love of power for its own sake, ill used, will ever come out to a good end nor establish itself permanently upon the earth.

This love of power, grown to Frankenstein proportions in occasional men of history, needs continually to be resisted by the common people of the world. As Wendell Phillips said: "Power is ever stealing from the many to the few. The manna of popular liberty must be gathered each day, or it is rotten."

No matter how great a man may be, there is no man on earth good enough to be trusted with unlimited power. It will not be good for his people and it will not be good for him. It is precisely at this point that some of us have such faith in democracy. It resists the tendency to put arbitrary power into the hands of one man. For the plain lesson of history is this, no one man has been able to handle unlimited power for the good of anybody except himself, and usually he has fallen on the sword of his own power.

Another kind of love that makes the world go round is the love of money, which is the root of all evil, according to Paul's letter to Timothy.

In the past we Americans have done business in tools of hell with anybody who wanted to buy for any purpose they might have. Why? Because there was money in it. Love of money will make a bandit kill a hermit for sixty-five cents, or love of money will let a business arm an enemy with guns to be later turned upon the seller, or love of money will lead a man to swindle widows and orphans and forge checks and sell worthless stock. The Bible is not far wrong, "The love of money is the root of all evil." And this kind of love for filthy lucre has made the world go round in circles these latter days. It will seem hard to believe what Thoreau says, "Money is not required to buy one necessity of the soul." Even Thoreau would admit that a little money is needed to buy a few necessities for the body. Someone has said that our incomes are like our shoes, if too small they pinch us; but if too large they cause us to stumble and to trip.

But there are other loves that can sweeten life beyond measure. The love of nature, the outer world of wild ducks flying, white clouds drifting, mountains shouldering out the sky, valleys white with winter or green with summer. You remember Lord Byron:

> There is a pleasure in the pathless woods,
> There is a rapture on the lonely shore,
> There is society where none intrudes
> By the deep sea, and music in its roar.

This afternoon, when your dinner is digested and

your nap is over, take up your hat and walk out into the world God made. Lift up your head and straighten up your spine, you are lord of all you survey and king of the land. It is yours for the seeing. The sky is yours for the asking. The love of nature can make your world go round with power to heal the hurts and mend the heart.

And what shall we say of the love of music making the world go round? Here is a girl who practises her piano five hours each day, not for the money in it but for the joy of it. That music makes her world go round. She would die without it.

On 42nd Street in New York one Wednesday night it was cold. Suddenly I heard a voice, clear and strong, coming out of the night. Soon I saw him, a negro standing in the shadow singing an aria from an Italian opera. "How old are you?" I asked when he had finished one of the finest songs I have ever heard. "Eighteen," he answered. A street singer at eighteen.

"But why do you sing outdoors on a cold night? For the money?"

"No," he explained to me, "not for the money, but I love to sing, and at home in the crowded tenement it bothers some people, they can't sleep, so I come outdoors, here, where nobody minds if I sing. I hope to do better, and get my chance, some time." The love of music is making the world go round for that boy on 42nd Street and for thousands like him for whom music hath charms.

How shall I speak of other loves, the love of painting, the love of good reading and writing, the love of manual creation in the shop or hobby corner? All these can make the world go round, for someone.

The last, and the first, great love that makes the world go round is the love of God Himself. All other loves merge and come to climax in this, the love of God, so much wider than the measure of man's mind.

It's love that makes the world go round.

WASHINGTON, JACK OF ALL TRADES

How that name Washington has woven itself into the fabric of our living! We have a Washington state and nearly every state has a Washington town and nearly every town in America has a Washington Street or a Washington Park or a Washington monument. You just cannot get far away from that straight-backed man riding in dignity on his white horse.

Today I want you to mark with me the variety and the intensity of the vocational interests of that human dynamo, George Washington. He was a jack of all trades and a master of most of them. Still a boy of only sixteen, he had mastered the intricacies of surveying and had roamed the wilderness reaches west of the Potomac. The Baltimore and Ohio Railroad later followed a route he had surveyed across the mountains. George was no pampered tea-hound as a youth. He could stand up and take it in all kinds of weather. Here is his personal diary, telling of a return trip from the Upper Ohio in 1753, when he was just twenty-one. "I determined to make my journey the nearest way through the woods, on foot. With gun in hand and pack on my back, I set out with Mr. Gist. The day following, we met up with a party of French Indians, who had lain in wait for us. One of them fired at Mr. Gist, or me, not 15 steps off, but fortunately missed. We took this fellow into custody and kept him until about 9 o'clock at night, then let him go, and walked all the remaining part of the night without making any stop, so as to be out of the reach of the pursuit of the Indians the next day, since we were well assured that they would follow our track as soon as it was light. The next day we hurried until quite dark and got to the river Allegheny. We expected to find the river frozen, but it was not.

"There was no way for getting over but on a raft, which we set about making with but one poor hatchet. This was a whole day's work. Then we set off, but before we were half way over, we were jammed in the ice, in such a manner that we expected every moment our raft to sink, and ourselves to perish. I put out my pole to try to stop the raft that the ice might pass by, when the rapidity of the stream threw it with so much violence against the pole, that it jerked me out into ten feet of water. But I fortunately saved myself by catching hold of one of the raft logs. We could not get to either shore and were obliged to make for an island where we stayed all night. Mr. Gist had all his fingers and some of his toes frozen. The next morning the river was frozen and we crossed to the shore and made our way to Mr. Frazier's."

Now this exciting story of just one minor excitement in the life of George Washington shows his aptitude in the wilderness, his ability, learned early, to meet every crisis calmly and skilfully. The old saying that "the brave die young," is not true for G. Washington because he had that tremendous will to live and plenty of good luck born more of courage than luck. And Washington's excellent diaries and state papers prove his power as a writer of the English language. He had no ghost writer to make up pretty phrases for him at five cents a word. The evidence is fairly clear that without radio or many newspapers, Washington was the most widely cultured and best informed man of the colonial period. He had that glorious insatiable curiosity for everything he saw and read that is the background of all intense learning.

Of course, the two obvious professions in which Washington excelled were military strategy and statesmanship. Lafayette testifies that he had never seen such calm, masterful leadership in battle as Washington showed under fire. Washington made mistakes, and he was the first to admit them, but somehow he knew how to keep from making the same mistake twice, and that is victory indeed. As for Washington, the statesman, little that I can say will add to the glory of the man, but do you remember what he said when some of his soldiers naively suggested that Washington should become King of America? It was in 1782 that Colonel Lewis Nicola dared suggest the monarchical title to his chief.

Washington came as near to visible anger in his refusal as I have ever read. "You could not have found a person," says Washington, "to whom your suggestion could be more disagreeable. Let me conjure you then, if you have any regard for your country, concern for yourself, or regard for me, to banish these thoughts from your mind." So the idea of Washington as king fell flat because the man most concerned was enough of a statesman to squash the idea at the very start. He was a statesman big enough to keep himself a servant of his country, not a master.

But once Washington did stand on the dignity of his office as President. It was in Boston in 1789, and involved a diplomatic duel with the proud Governor Hancock of Massachusetts. Hancock was determined to make the President call on the Governor first instead of vice versa, thus making Washington admit the supremacy of the State over the Federal government. Hancock worked it in this way, he sent a note to Washington's lodgings complaining of the gout, and would Washington call on Hancock? The President sent his sympathy to Hancock by messenger but did not choose to disturb the Governor by calling in his illness. The next day Hancock relented and said that he would risk his health to call on the President. Hancock arrived in his gorgeous coach, had his servants carry him into Washington's presence, where Washington greeted him with the hope that the journey had not hazarded the Governor's health. Hancock had not wasted any love on Washington since the day that John Adams had proposed Washington as commander in chief instead of naming Hancock, who very much wanted the post. The Boston incident marks the first defeat in American history of states rights in conflict with national sovereignty.

So far we have noted Washington the surveyor, the hardy frontiersman, the military genius, the statesman *par excellence.*

But that is not the end of his versatility, by any means. As squire of Mount Vernon he was a farmer who knew his lands better than most plantation owners. And Washington was probably the first scientific farmer in America. Tobacco had been the main crop in Virginia, but tobacco drained the soil of its fertility and Washington introduced various kinds of wheat, selling six thousand bushels in 1769. He invented an improved plow. He developed the now accepted idea of rotation of crops and at his death he left written plans for the rotation of crops at Mount Vernon up to 1803.

And to add one more trade, he enjoyed fishing just as much as any disciple of Isaac Walton who is this very day looking over his reels and flies. One day in May, when he was thirty-six years old, he writes in his diary, "Fishing for sturgeon on the York River, from breakfast to dinner, but catched none." So he may not have been a master of fishing, just an apprentice.

There was much of the prophet and reformer in

Washington, too. He is roundly condemned for holding slaves, but if all slave holders had been as kindly as Washington, slavery would not have been the vicious evil it became after his day. In 1794, Washington could say something very much ahead of his time, "Were it not then, that I am principled against selling negroes, as you would cattle at a market, I would not in twelve months be possessed of one as a slave. I shall be mistaken if they are not found to be very troublesome species of property ere many years pass over our heads."

And on many another subject Washington was as farsighted as on slavery. In 1793 Washington granted permission to Pierre Blanchard of France for a balloon ascension in Philadelphia. Nine years earlier Washington had written in a private letter, "I have only newspaper accounts of air balloons. The tales relating to them are marvelous and lead us to expect that our friends at Paris in a little time will come flying through the air instead of ploughing the ocean to get to America."

And to move from the upper air down into the water, we think of the submarine as a modern device. Washington slept on the dock in New York one night in 1776 while the first submarine in New York harbor tried to sink Admiral Howe's flagship, the *Eagle*. It was a small submarine built by a Mr. Bushnell and was lighter than the water displaced when submerged. It was forced under water by a vertical propeller and driven forward by a horizontal one. Both were operated by hand cranks. One Ezra Lee drove the submarine out toward the British flagship with a bomb attached to the bottom, but the bomb blew up one hundred feet from the ship and Washington dragged the half drowned patriot out of the water.

This man Washington was ahead of his time.

Somebody will ask you if you believe the story about the cherry tree. And did Washington ever tell a lie? These are not the important points. Here is the glory of these stories. They are told about a man of whom they *could* be true. He was that kind of man, a man who commonly spoke the truth. He was not known as a liar. His word could be depended upon, so the story grew up that he never told a lie. That is a nice reputation to have. All of us give our family and friends a general impression of our character, or lack of it. And we get to be known as that kind of person. One man is marked for his honesty in every dealing, as was Washington. Another man is known for his sympathy and kindliness, as was Lincoln. Another man is known for his brutality, as is Hitler. A woman may be known for her grace and beauty. Another woman may be known for her cruelty, like Jezebel. We are known by the general tone and quality of our conduct, day in and day out. And that is as it should be.

George Washington was the kind of man who was great enough to be first in the hearts of his countrymen.

NOW COMES HOLY WEEK

FROM a window on Beacon Street I see that we are on the threshold of Holy Week in a year when the world could use a week of holiness the way a drowning man could use a bagful of fresh air.

Holy Week! Does that mean anything to you or is it merely a vague title for the week when you buy a new hat with gloves to match? Holy Week could mean something very deep and very important to you and me, something more than a new suit and a box of candy for Easter.

For one thing Holy Week could help us forget our own troubles by taking a good look at somebody else who got into more trouble in one week than we are likely to face in one lifetime, and that somebody was Jesus. When we begin to pity ourselves because we are lonely in the middle of the big city, it may help to look at Jesus in the big city of Jerusalem before Pontius Pilate. Jesus, so lonely that even his closest friends had skipped town to get out of trouble, the while Jesus was getting into deeper and deeper trouble. The plain truth is that Jesus was so lonely on Friday of that first Holy Week that he thought even God had forsaken him. So if you are living in solitude now, take all the comfort you can get out of the clear fact that Jesus lost more friends in three days than most of us could lose in a year. Or if your sorrow is that almost nobody understands you, your hopes and fears and purposes and weaknesses, take courage this Holy Week from the evidence that nobody understood Jesus either, when he talked about the Kingdom of God. They thought him possessed of a devil and mocked him and crucified him. Why? Because they did not understand him until it was too late. That is what usually happens to the people who are either too bad or too good for this world which loves average mediocrity. We crucify the criminals and the saints. Then later we try to make up for our mistake by worshipping the saints. And the closer you live to the spirit of Jesus the more likely it is that you will be misunderstood too in a world which is not ready to live his way.

So on the days of this Holy Week when you begin to feel sorry for yourself, ask yourself these questions. Did you ever hear a mob crying for your crucifixion? Jesus did. Have you ever had a crown of thorns pressed into your head until the blood fell on your face? Jesus did. Have you ever been spat upon with malice aforethought? Jesus was. Have you ever been condemned to death and then had to carry your own means of torture to the death place? This happened to Jesus. And a lot more happened to him that is not likely to happen to you. Take heart then, if you are in trouble, you are in good company. Jesus was in trouble too.

A second truth that Holy Week illustrates is that often good people have to take the punishment for the mistakes the bad people make. It happened at Calvary; it happened before Calvary; it happens today. Jesus, in whom Pilate could find no fault, gets hung up on a tree to die, and Barabbas, a murderer, goes free. That certainly does not look like justice. But then I wonder how Barabbas felt the rest of his life, knowing that his freedom meant the death of Christ. It probably never bothered him. The only justice is the verdict of history, that Jesus, taking the punishment for other men's mistakes, is more loved and admired than any person who ever has walked this earth, and Barabbas is known for what he was, a criminal who got off lightly. And I know of no church called after Barabbas, I know of no mother, who since that day, has named her son Barabbas. Thus justice catches up with injustice in the long run, but in the short sprint a lot of innocent people get hurt. When you see a wife holding her family together in spite of the desertion of a profligate husband, you see a woman taking the punishment for another's mistakes, the way Jesus did.

Late at night not long ago a man was killed out here on Beacon Street by a careening car driven by a drunken fool. The pedestrian tried to dodge the crazy car but the car seemed to chase after him, haul him down and strike him dead. The driver gets off about as easily as Barabbas, but the pedestrian sacri-

fices his life cut down short in its prime. The driver
gets a short sentence, but the innocent pedestrian
gets a long sentence, for eternity—killed by another
man's mistake.

Not long ago a consignment of powerful drugs
came out of a New York factory with a deadly poison
put into the formula by mistake. Before that consignment could be called back the drug had killed
half a dozen people in various corners of the country.
There it is again, somebody killed by another person's mistake. The tragedy is not only that it happened to Jesus but that it happens all around us almost every day in one way or another, that even
though few innocent people are completely killed by
mistake, they are often terribly hurt in body, mind
or soul. And it happens in public ways too, as well
as private. Who gets hurt in modern war? Is it Hitler in his mountain retreat, the man who plans the
war? Does he get hurt? Hardly. He eats three square
meals a day and has a bodyguard to protect the hairs
of his head. And yet his mistaken leadership con-
demns innocent children in London and Berlin to
starvation and death as horrible as that which Jesus
suffered. Holy Week is not something in ancient history, it is vivid with contemporary meaning and as
fresh as this morning's sunlight. You cannot escape
it forever. Some time, somewhere, somehow, innocent victims suffer terribly for the mistakes that other
people make. No easy going pollyanna philosophy

of life can escape that fact. But who wants to escape? Jesus did not run away from Calvary, he walked toward it, unafraid. Sometimes that is all you can do, and keep faith with your own best self.

Something else that Holy Week can do for us is to remind us of just what holiness really is. Some people think of holiness as a kind of ethereal piety lived in seclusion away from the temptations of daily life. Holiness may be that, to be sure, but it is also something else. The very word "holy," as we use it, comes from an Anglo-Saxon root, "hal," meaning complete, whole, entire. Then holiness at its best means that your personality is complete. You are not half a man. Or as the psychiatrists would say, you are integrated, entire, put together as a unit. Now if holiness means this completeness of personality, it means that in Holy Week we have the responsibility of trying to become whole again after living partially and fractionally. If your days are bound up with what you eat and drink, and how you feel and what you wear, you are living a fractional life, incomplete because things of the mind and spirit have been lost to your own impoverishment. This Holy Week for you can be a week of completion if you will give your mind as much attention as you do your body, and your soul as much food as you do your stomach. There used to be a saying that an army moves on its stomach. That is only half true. Army officers now say that an army moves on its stomach and its morale, by which they mean that if soldiers do not believe in the cause they fight for, they will be poor soldiers no matter how well fed they may be. "Man shall not live by bread alone" is as true today as when Jesus said it first. But maybe it is your mind that is getting too much work, while you miss the sunset over the western hills and are so busy you do not have time to take a walk along the river. That is too bad, because then your life is incomplete. Overweighted on the intellectual side you are in danger of losing the simple joys of sight and sound and taste. No matter how brilliant you become intellectually or spiritually you ought to keep your interest in a good dinner. You have to eat, so why not enjoy it?

It is this harmonizing of the mind and spirit and body that makes for strong character and radiant personality. Where anyone is neglected trouble is sure to follow. And Holy Week says clearly, "Stop being a fraction and become an integer."

Holy Week also says to us that once in a while we have to put aside a week to set our souls straight in the midst of a crooked generation. Now someone will say that it should be Holy Year instead of Holy Week, or Holy Day. Holiness ought to be a constant goal instead of a temporary excitement during one week of the year. So. But we human beings are so put together that we have to have seasons for doing some things. We ought to know enough to do without seasonal emphasis. We all ought to write to our friends more than we do to bespeak our love and

affection, but we do not do it, so we have the Christmas Season, a week when we can tell our friends we
still think of them. We ought always to be grateful
for the freedom and democracy of our America, but
we have the Fourth of July when we really get excited about it and set off fireworks by day and by
night to concentrate into a few hours our gratitude
for freedom. So we ought always to be thankful, but
knowing that what is generally true may not come
true in particular we set aside at least one day of the
year for Thanksgiving.

So we have a better homes week, which often
seems more concerned with better furnaces in the
cellar than better husbands in the parlor. And we
have an apple week and buy-a-new-car week and a
national bread week and a better babies week and
a fire prevention week and a call-the-policeman
week and a clean-up-the-streets week. And I suppose
we need them all to remind us of some things we
might otherwise forget.

This, then, is Holy Week. And that means, surely,
that we take a long look at Jesus, then another look
at our own personal daily living. It ought to be a
week of honest checking up on ourselves, of taking
our crosses instead of running around them and
making excuses. It ought to be a week of coming
back to God if we are far from God. Each of us will
know what that means, something very personal,
something very needed, something very hard, perchance, something that will make a big difference in

the way we live with other people and may make a big difference in the world around us.

May Holy Week find us climbing uphill instead of sliding downhill.

RENEWAL

FROM my window I have been watching the Easter Parade. I can report that the newest thing in hats is the patriotic motif with red, white and blue rampant over colored straw set on the head at an acute angle.

But it is not new things for Easter, but renewed things for Easter that I want to write about today, for somehow, my old felt hat comes off not so much to the people who buy new clothes for Easter as to the people who renew their clothes for Easter. I see a girl who works in an office and supports her mother too. She has what looks like a new hat today, but she confesses that it is five years old, not new at all, only a renewed arrangement of a little ribbon and a few artificial flowers on straw. But her skill with something renewed makes it look like something new.

The other day a husband tried to reprove his wife by saying, "Didn't I hear you tell your friends that your party dress came from abroad?" His wife explained, "Not exactly, dear. You see, it's last year's dress which I turned inside out. I simply said, 'It's from the other side.'"

So more dresses than we might guess on Easter Day are "from the other side." They are not as new

as they look. They are renewed. Anybody can have
something new, if he can get the money; but how
deeply we admire the people who make over old
things to look like new by the very skill born of
their poverty.

For more than we think, life demands of us the
power of renovation more than the novelty of inno-
vation. In the 51st Psalm we catch a glimpse of this
truth very clearly when the cry goes up to God, "Renew a right spirit within me." The point is obvious,
you and I cannot ask for brand new spirits fresh
out of the department store. The best we can hope
is that our old spirits can be made over, renewed,
restored, renovated, on the principle that deep within
the soul of every man and woman there is a nucleus
of sound rightness waiting to be fed and enlarged and
encouraged. The truth is that no one is so hopeless but
that deep within his own soul God still lives, though
He may be imprisoned and strangled. In a world
where wrong spirits get hold of us, both alcoholic
and demonic, when our souls are captured by defeat-
ism, by fear, by jealousy, by worry, we do well to
pray, "O God, renew a right spirit within me."

And the plain truth is that most of the great
things we all want have to be renewed rather than
purchased fresh wrapped in cellophane.

Here is this piece of impedimenta each of us carries around with us, called a human body. How many
people would like to order a new one and turn in the
old model. But we cannot. Nevertheless we can pray,

"Renew a right body around me." And by the way we live, in good health disciplines, we can help to answer that prayer and get a renewed body. The New Testament is full of almost miraculous accounts of people whose bodies were renewed because they believed it could happen to them. I am no cultist about faith cures but I have seen too many people get better physically because they *believed* they could get better, to laugh at any religion or any doctor who tries to renew human bodies. We need not stay the way we are, spiritually or physically. When Isaiah talks about those who wait on the Lord "renewing their strength," he is declaring that renewal is a fact and not a fiction.

Somebody today is looking for a new job. You have tired of the old routine and you are weary of the five o'clock whistle. You may both need and deserve a new job, but until you get it here is a good prayer, "Renew my old job so that I shall see it as part of a larger plan and think of myself as working for God and the world, not alone for myself." Everybody gets tired of an old job once in a while, then it has to be renewed. For the certain testimony is that the people who stay with an old job and renew it, do better work more joyfully than the people who jump from pillar to post, from one job to another without finding permanent skill or joy.

Somebody else is saying that we need a new kind of government in this country, a new order copied after the brutal dictatorships of Central Europe. I

protest that it is not a new order we need, but we do
need a renewed faith in the democracy we have tried
to maintain here for one hundred and fifty years.
Old things need to be renewed, and our faith in
the democratic way of life desperately needs renewal
right now. And how will that renewal be made manifest? By our working as hard to make democratic
ideals regnant in daily life as the dictators do to
make their lack of ideals all powerful in the people
under their heels. Unless our kind of government is
renewed from within, it will be impossible to save
it from destruction from without. O God, renew a
right spirit within America.

But what is this I hear? Someone asking for new
friends after having lost all the old ones. New friends
are surely very exciting, but the old counsel is still
good, "The friends thou hast and their adoption
tried, grapple them to thy soul with hoops of steel."
Something is very certainly wrong with the man or
woman who loses friends so fast he has to make new
ones to have any at all. And that something is very
serious, for friendships should grow deeper and
richer with the years, even though letters may be
scarce and visits with each other rarely possible. Some
of the loneliest people I know are secretly praying
that they will meet new and glamorous and wonderful friends. Here is a better prayer, "O God, renew
the old friendships that I have let fall into careless
decay." "Renew some right friendships, beginning
within me."

Another place where we often long for newness and really need renewal is in our homes. Our family would do so much better if we could live in a new house, we say, or buy some new furniture, or perchance have a new father, or a new husband or a new wife, or a new father-in-law. If only we could start over with all things new, then they would be different. But would they? Granted that if the old house is a fire trap in a slum you need a new apartment in a housing project, still for most of us it is not so much new homes that we need, it is renewed homes. So that when we houseclean, we had better sweep out not only the cobwebs but also the animosities and the bickerings and the misunderstandings and the double dealing. It seems to me the very destiny of our days is bound up with what happens in our homes, more than what happens anywhere else, simply because we are at home longer hours than anywhere else, or should be. If home is the place we get away from, then something is wrong with that home, and we need to pray, "Renew a right spirit within our house, beginning with me."

Just how do you renew a home? Is it only a matter of a little overtime work for the vacuum cleaner? It is something more than that. Renewing a home is bringing laughter and joy back where sulkiness has been. Renewing a home is helping each other with the chores and thinking up games after supper and having company in for a song-fest. Renewing a home is sharing each other's joys and tears and making that little shack or mighty palace the dearest place on earth. That is what home should be.

The last new thing I see somebody looking for is a new religion. Boston's Back Bay has in it, by actual count, some sixty-three varieties of religion. Almost all these "varieties of religious experience" as William James called them are sincere in their search for truth and may I say that almost any one of them, followed through in careful discipline and faithful devotion, will lead very near to God and truth and inner peace and power. Why should there be so many kinds of religion? Simply because there are so many kinds of people.

But this is the point, it takes time to get deep into any profound religion. You cannot catch religion as you do the measles and be over it in two weeks if that religion is to help your daily living. And yet there are people who drift from one church to another and from one cult to another looking for what they never seem to find, a new religion that will answer all their questions and set them at ease in Zion.

To all such people the word comes clear and strong, "You do not need a new religion so much as you need a renewed religion. You need a renewal of the power that is in the old religion you have known before. For religion at its best is not in a church, it is in us, deep in our own souls, and until we find it there we find it nowhere."

I hope you have something new this Easter, but more than that, may you have something renewed.

THE WISHING WELL

I STOLE an afternoon out of the last day of winter and jumped the gun on the springtime by going to the Flower Show.

The bitter cold, blustery wind of March was on the outside of the door, but inside, at the Flower Show, the fragrance of azalea and rose almost blew you down. An acacia grove, in every possible shade of yellow, with a waterfall in the midst, was the end piece of incomparable beauty. Formal rose gardens in full bloom seemed like a dream from another world, a picnic grove seemed ready for the Fourth of July even now, and seeds were being bought by the bushel by people who seem to believe with Shelley that, "If winter comes, can spring be far behind?" There was very little spring outdoors but the air was full of it inside.

But let me tell you about the most popular spot in the whole show, and that place was not a flower exhibit. It was the wishing well, set right in the center of things, an old stone replica of the wishing well at Canterbury Cathedral, with the old oaken bucket hanging on an iron grill above the well. A little sign said that money dropped into the wishing well that day would be given to Norwegian War Relief.

Everybody seemed to want to make a wish, leaning

over the brink of that well, and everybody seemed to want to drop a coin into the well to help with war relief. And not coins only, for I saw a five dollar bill and a basketful of other lesser bills at the bottom of that wishing well. You see it costs something to make your wish come true.

And then I stood by and listened to the wishes people made as they spoke their fervent prayers at the brim of the wishing well. Usually they would pause a moment, coin in hand, as if wondering just what the most important wish in the world could be. Then a flash of decision would pass over their faces, the coin would plunk into the echoing depths, and the wish was made and paid for. Now all it had to do was come true. I am sure that the deepest wishes were unspoken, far down in the hidden places of the heart where no other heart could know. But a lot of wishing was being done by that well, I am sure of that. I saw a pale, intense, Norwegian refugee step up to the well and say with bated breath, "I wish for the complete defeat of the Axis powers." Her neighbor added, "I'll put in my fifty cents to make that wish come true."

Soon a lovely English child, now seeking refuge in America, dropped her coin and said with a charming English accent, "I wish the war would be over and I could go home to Daddy." There was a hush at the brim of the wishing well and a lot of wishes joined hers. It may cost something to make that wish come true.

Then, in vivid contrast, I asked a husky American boy about eleven what he had wished for and he answered, "I didn't wish for anything because I don't need anything." His mother explained that he put his coin in the well just the same, because the Norwegian children did need something, very certainly.

Now right at the brim of this wishing well at the Flower Show we are face to face with very pointed truths for our personal and public living in a world like this.

For one thing, making a wish is not the superstitious fol-de-rol some people think. It can be the very stuff out of which our future action is made. If, as Elizabeth Barrett Browning said, "Every wish is like a prayer with God," then we have to be careful what we wish for, for we may surely get that wish. Certainly no strong personal character ever comes to the soul that does not wish for it at the beginning. Our wish determines the course of our conduct, the kind of lives we live, and it makes a great deal of difference what we wish for. You may inherit a fine house or a diamond ring or a fur coat without wishing for it, but the good things of the mind and soul cannot be handed down from one generation to another quite so easily. If you want to be a master in your profession you will have to wish for mastery so hard that you are willing to pay to make that wish come true by hard work. If you want to be clean hearted you will have to wish for a clean heart so hard that your conduct begins to make that wish come true.

Here we are near the Lenten season with its emphasis on improved personal character. To some people this season will mean everything because, wishing to be better men and women, they will wish to conquer some sin and acquire new character and, wishing it hard, they will pay the price to make that wish come true by decisive forsaking of old evil ways. To other people Lent means less than nothing simply because they do not have any great desire, any deep-going, soul-stirring wish to be better than they are. Here is a question to give each of us pause any day, "What am I really wishing for myself? Is it something I ought to have? And am I paying the price of making that wish come true?"

Here is a man who is working as a kitchen hand in a big restaurant. He tells me he wishes he had a better job. But I tell him his wishing is only skin deep because he is not studying nights to get ready for a better job. He is not ready to do any other work well, so his wishing is half-hearted. There is another wish he could make, and that is a wish that even among the pots and pans of his kitchen he might find the presence of God, as Brother Lawrence did. If he cannot get a better job, he can make the job he has better. He can put into it more imagination, more driving purpose. He can see that kitchen as almost his altar, his shrine, where good food, well cooked, is his votive offering to hungry men and women, and his pots can shine with the glory of the Lord. That has happened and it is happening right now in millions of kitchens where men and women are doing the dishes and thanking God they have had food on the dishes.

In the next place it is wiser to wish for qualities of character than for money as such. The rather bitter story of "The Monkey's Paw" is a tragic reminder that it may take tragedy to make some of our wishes come true. The story is about a monkey's paw that would grant any wish made while rubbing its smooth fur. A man and his wife decide to wish for two hundred pounds to pay off a debt and be financially clear. The wish is made with the help of the monkey's paw and they wonder where the two hundred pounds will come from. They have only a few hours to wait, for their son has been working at the mill. In the late afternoon an investigator from the mill arrives with bad news. The boy has been killed in a mill accident and the company offers to settle the case for—two hundred pounds. So the monkey's paw becomes not the giver of joy it was supposed to be, but the precursor of tragedy because it costs so much to make its wishes come true.

What are we wishing for today? Each of us right now? I can guess what millions of us human beings all over the world are wishing as we step up to the brim of the wishing well. For one thing, almost everybody wishes to be loved by someone. If you have never wished that you are a little abnormal. No matter what else we have, if nobody loves us we sing the plaintive prisoner's song, "Oh, I wish I had someone to love me, for I'm tired of living alone." Now let us look at that wish and ask, Are you willing to pay the price of having that wish come true? For here it is, as surely as night follows day, if you give out from your own heart the kind of love you wish for, deep, loyal, full, that love will come back to you from somewhere, some time. Of course I know that every girl and every man who wishes for romantic love does not find it. But even so, it is better to have loved and lost than never to have loved at all. And experience is clear at this point, that unrequited romantic love, turned to higher forms of love for people who need that love desperately, never does go out unreturned. It is only when unreturned love grows bitter and hard and introspective and selfish that such love stays unreturned forever. Anyone who wants to be loved can be loved, if he will pay the price of giving love where it is needed.

Or somebody else says that above all else he wishes for work. That is a good wish and a common wish. And that wish need never go unfulfilled because any man or woman who will pay the price of becoming skilled to do one job superbly well will not go without work for long. Just wishing for work will not get it, but the wish, followed by burning the midnight oil to make oneself ready for a job, will make that wish come true.

Or here is somebody wishing for an education. The wish alone will not get it, but if, when you step up to the wishing well and make that wish, you also prom-mise to pay the price of making that wish come true, night school, home study, hard discipline, then your wish is the beginning of hopes fulfilled for you.

Often people tell me they wish they could see God. They have looked for him everywhere and found only vacancy. The hope of making that wish come true is that God is not far from any one of us. He is nearer than breathing, closer than hands or feet. God was in the blossoms at the Flower Show. God is in the lengthening days so soon to bring spring back to our cold earth. God is in the face of a child, if you will see him there. God is in your conscience telling you this is right and that is wrong, if you will hear his voice. God is working his way in the comedy or tragedy of your own daily life. Look for him right there and you will see him.

What is *my* wish? That if your wishes are good for you and the world, they may all come true.

TIME AND ETERNITY

I SEE that we are living today, the first day of daylight saving, on a time schedule one hour earlier than yesterday. We have taken time by the forelock and pulled it ahead one hour so that, although we lost an hour's sleep last night, we get an extra hour of daylight this evening. And just such a little thing as turning our watches and clocks ahead one hour can tell us a great deal about ourselves and the world we live in.

The first thing we see clearly is that we can change our habits when we really have to and when everybody else is changing too. We all know we ought to get up an hour earlier and get busy when the day is fresh and the air clear. But such creatures of habit are we that we do not do what we ought to do unless something wakes us up and changes our habits overnight, like daylight saving. The first day it seems hard to get up early, but soon we get used to it and we like getting up early because it gives us a better day.

So it is with any habit which gets a hold on us until we cannot see how to break its spell; what we need is something to stab us wide awake and help us save ourselves before it is too late. Some of us have fallen

into the habit of doing slovenly work, just getting by
at school or the office or the shop. What we need is
a personal declaration of work-saving that will snap
us out of that rut and put a finer touch in our hands
and a high quality into our work. We can turn the
quality of our work ahead just as surely as we can
turn our clocks ahead, although not quite so easily,
to be sure.

Or I see someone else who has fallen into the habit
of indecision, putting off till another day the actions
that should be performed today. That indecision can
eat away a man's backbone quicker than acid and
make him a jellyfish walking on two legs. The only
way I know to snap out of that rut of indecision is to
snap out of it, to begin to decide little things and
then big things, and then to act on those decisions.
Amiel, in his self-revealing Journal, says, "I am always practising, but never performing." Always thinking things over, but never thinking things through to
a decision, is a habit that takes something like an explosion to get us out of. But how we need it sometimes.

Or look at a habit like fear, how that can shrivel
up the soul and leave us in torment day and night.
Nothing but a great faith in something strong enough
to overcome our fears will save us then. And until we
find that faith we are lost on the mountains in the
rain.

Then what shall we say when habits, like vulgarity
or alcoholism, get their octopus grip on a soul that

was intended for something finer than lewd jokes and week-end benders and staggers? Is there any character saving as well as daylight saving for a life in the hellish grip of a bad habit? There was for the prodigal son, and for Augustine, and for a million more who have been wakened out of their sin before it was too late, wakened by looming tragedy, or inner soul sickness finally disgusted with itself. Or sometimes the love and counsel of a good friend has conquered a bad habit and made a new beginning. It can happen to you and me. That is what religion is all about, a life-changing power. Daylight saving says that when we really want to we can change our habits for the better and get up early instead of late, begin to live for the right instead of the wrong, tell the truth instead of lies, live for mercy instead of brutality. If we can change our clocks, why not change our lives? We can if we will. But it takes a lot of willing and a deep inner desire to be changed for the better.

Something else we see clearly today, as we think of time and eternity, is that time is the most evenly distributed commodity in the world. You have exactly as much time per day as every other person in the world. You may not have as much money as the man next door. You may not be as handsome as your cousin, you may not live in a mansion like your uncle's, but you have as much time as Aristotle did to think deeply about life and truth, you have as much time as Edison did to invent new designs for living, you have as much time as Lincoln did to read the Bible and Milton and Shakespeare. Let no man ever say, "I haven't much time." He has all there is, every day. And the saddest people I know are the people who say they have time on their hands and do not know what to do with it. Here in a world that needs all the Red Cross knitting we can do, a world that needs the tools of peace surely as much as it needs the tools of war, a world with books to be read, diseases to be healed, friendships to be maintained, letters to be written, for anyone to say he or she has time to waste, is to say that the soul is empty of resources and the mind is already dead and ready to be buried. In a world full of the music of bombs or symphonies, of dying men or laughing children, we need never say we cannot hear anything at all, unless we are deaf. In a world full of beauty and ugliness, comedy and tragedy on every street, we need never complain we have nothing to look at. The other day I saw blind men working hard all day making mattresses in a factory, doing it all by touch and skilled technical understanding. I saw blind girls sewing the seams on the mattress covers, busy as the day is long. And when they go home at night on the street cars the conductors help them find their way through the intricacies of the subway system. They have no time on their hands to waste, because they have filled the flying minutes with work and life to the full. There is no other way to live, worth living. Whenever we say we are killing time, we are wrong. We cannot kill time; time kills us.

Now do not misunderstand me, I believe that every day should have time in it for relaxed laughter, but that is not killing time, that is making it live. No life can be well shaped unless it has in it four very clear elements. First there must be work, hard work through the good hours of the day. Without it we sink into self-shame and parasitism, taking out of life more than we put into it. So that unless we are sick we miss the first purpose of our existence if we do not fill the best hours of the day with unremitting work, well done, for the joy of it as much as for the money in it. Then there must be time in each day for friendship so that the day is not done unless we have someone to love or care for.

And we must take time for play, too, for that is not time wasted which relaxes body and mind. It may be only a few minutes a day, but it may save the mind from breakdown. And let there be time in each day for moments of reverence in the presence of something greater than we are, the majesty of God, the beauty of nature, the character of Jesus. And in addition to these four, there should be time to eat wisely and to sleep quietly. A life lived to the full with time for work and friendship, play and worship, will never be a life that has to kill time. The hours will be all too short for the fulfillment of plans. And that is the way it should be. As Thoreau put it, "You cannot kill time without injuring eternity." Or in Shakespeare's phrasing, "I wasted time, and now doth time waste me."

Still another truth worth remembering on this first day of daylight saving is that some things are better done early than late. A stitch in time saves nine. "It is later than you think." A few weeks ago in a Massachusetts village, the town fathers voted to postpone burning the marsh grass at a cost of $300. Not many days after that postponement the dry marsh grass caught fire, a high wind spread the flames to the near-by houses and before the fire blew out to sea, $1,000,000 worth of property had been destroyed. So $300 spent in time would have saved $1,000,000 lost too late to be saved.

It is so all through our public and private life. A disease caught early will perchance save a life. A mistake corrected early will prevent a worse mistake later. A decision made on time will stop a mistake made too late. A hatred healed early will prevent a rupture when it is too late to heal.

The last clear help we find today is that time is a great healer. More than we sometimes guess the wounds of outrageous fortune will heal over in the days to come, and what seemed a wound that would bleed forever may be only a faint scar after time has done its healing work.

Remember that when you are hurt badly, in body or soul—time is a great healer. "This too will pass away," is the truest thing ever said about our troubles.

Dr. Cabot calls this healing power of time, "Vis Medicatrix Dei," the healing power of God.

So if your heart has been broken, believe that time

can heal that break and put your heart together again. If life has taken the dearest person you know, remember that time can heal that wound, too. If you have made a big mistake and wonder how you can live face to face with your own miserable self, remember that time and forgiveness will heal that hurt too, and one day you will face the morning light made over in a better mould, unafraid. Count greatly on the healing power of time.

In baseball and golf and tennis the experts talk a great deal about proper timing, by which they mean that you meet the ball at just the right instant for the right result. So in life, our conduct is as much a matter of timing as it is of power.

WHAT MAKES A HOUSE A HOME?

ALL OF us think about one dear place more than any other—home. The home we remember in the good old days, the home we live in now, full of life and laughter and once in a while a tear, or the home we hope to have in a few years when the right man or the wonderful girl comes along.

Many of you who work in the big city have gone home to mother on Mother's Day, and just your being home says more than anything you might put into words, and she understands. It is strange but true, that living away from one's mother makes her gain a glamour and a reverence we seldom feel when with her. Now we understand the care she took in little things, the anxiety she felt if we were hurt. Now we miss being tucked into bed at night. This, then, is a day to remember, remember the things we ought not to forget, that somebody once took great pains to get us into this world, that somebody sang songs to put us into peaceful sleep on stormy nights, that somebody set out the clothes so we could go to school fresh and ready for a new, exciting day. You will hear some people say that this Mother's Day idea is sentimental slush. Well, it can be that if that is all there is to it. But it could be a lot more than that. And it is, when we remember some of the hopes mother had for us, and then try to live up to those hopes. It could be a great day if some of us remembered the prayers we heard her speak long years ago, and then tried to answer those prayers ourselves, by our conduct and by what we say and by what we are. Probably nobody ever fulfills all his mother's hopes for his life, but it is something to try for. And that trying is a long way from being sentimental slush. It is very close to plain, practical common sense.

We talk about this man-made world. If we men have made this world what it is today, in its tragedy, we might well be ashamed of ourselves and be sure that our wives and mothers and daughters might have done better. A matriarchal society might be preferable to a patriarchal. Women have an intuition that sees trouble ahead before it breaks, and they often know what to do about it, if men do not spoil their plans. Women have a capacity for indirect and subtle action that often wins its point more completely than the blundering, blustering, direct knock-'em-down and drag-'em-out ways that men are likely to use. Women have a capacity for forgiveness that heals wounds instead of rubbing salt into them. What I am trying to say is that our world would be better off if there were more mothers in particular and women in general given a chance to say how the world should be run. I have often felt that one of the things that is most wrong with Adolf Hitler is that he has no wife or daughter to give him a little good advice in the evening after work. It might have helped to save the world some trouble.

For if mothers had a chance to get the kind of world they would like, it would be a very different world from the one we have now.

For one thing, every mother wants her children to have enough plain food to grow into normal men and women. That does not seem like an unfair request and yet millions of men in many corners of the earth are watching their own children starve because there is no way to get the bountiful harvests into their hungry stomachs. If Mother's Day means anything at all it ought to mean that we men dedicate ourselves to making it possible for every mother in the world, black or white, yellow or brown, to see her children go to bed at night with a warm supper in their stomachs, instead of the gnawing torture of emptiness. What are we men going to do about that?

For another thing, every mother I have asked, has fervently declared her deep desire that her children shall not have to be blown to pieces in war. Mothers have asked me why we men cannot see war coming soon enough to stop it before it sets the whole world into thundering flame. And my answer? We are just too dumb to be able to figure it out. All we know how to do is to make more war in an attempt to end war. Then in another twenty-five years, when your son's sons are old enough to be soldiers, we will have another war for them to die in. If ever man, as the supposed *homo sapiens,* took pride in his own attainments, in airplanes and submarines and TNT and a hundred other wonderful inventions, he should hang his head in shame today, for we men have brought motherhood to a new low of security and calm stability and to a new high of terror that flieth by night.

Another hope that every mother has is that her children will have a fair chance at work they may come to enjoy and not hate. Being tied to a job you do not like is not only hard work, it is crass boredom. But the only way to be sure of making a living at a job you do enjoy is to learn the necessary skill for work you like and then work at that skill until you are so good at it that somebody will need what you can do. That means vocational guidance, that means school, that means study. Do we have what it takes?

And today when we are thinking naturally of home and family life it is wise to remind ourselves of what it is that makes a house a home. We all know there must be something besides a front door and a furnace in the cellar and a kitchen sink and a place to hang your hat. The other day in a suburb I passed a newly finished house fronted by a big sign, "This aristocratic home is for sale." But that was no home, for nobody lived in it. It was a house, no matter how aristocratic.

No house becomes a home, then, until somebody lives in it, gladly. If the house where you live is a boarding place that you go to just for the baked beans, brown bread and the night's sleep, that is good housing, maybe, but not good homing. A house is a place you go to when you have no other place. A home is the place you hurry to just as soon as you can get away from work. There is a big difference, and that difference is the difference between bare existtence and life—joyous life.

Then too, your house is not a home unless each person takes an interest in making that home liveable. Mother may do the housework, but father cleans the cellar and spades the garden and comes to love the place because he has put some work into it. And fifteen-year-old Sally calls it home partly because she painted the porch furniture yesterday and is right proud of the Nile green she got all over the furniture and on her pretty fingers. And ten-year-old Jimmy knows his house is home because he has to bring up the fireplace wood every Saturday morning and rake up the leaves each fall. We love most the people and the causes that we work the hardest for. That is why no house is a home until we can look at something around the place and remember, "I made that."

No house is ever a home until we help each other with the work around the place. The young husband who plunks down behind the sport page right after supper without offering to help his new wife with the dishes has not learned how to make that house a home, yet. So in any home worthy of the name, it is the give and take, but mostly give, that keeps the place from being a madhouse of each one grabbing for himself.

No house is a home unless the people who live there know how to play together in the long winter evenings. I venture the conviction that if any member of your family feels he has to go out every night in the week, he is making the place a house, not a home. At least once a week let the family get together around the parlor table and have a grand, hilarious time of it, with any game you happen to like, or a puzzle, or a round of good jokes, or good songs, or good books read and shared with each other. It is this having fun at home, with the neighbors in once in a while, that changes a house into a home.

Another test of whether where you live is a house or a home is the way you plan things ahead. If one of you, say the father or the mother, is a grim dictator who tells everybody else in the house what he or she is to do, that does not look like a home to me, it looks like a concentration camp. The best homes I know are the ones where the family talks things over and makes plans at the breakfast table, but the plans grow out of democratic conversation. They do not come down from the Lord High Almighty Pooh Bah, otherwise known as father. Of course once in a while he lays down the law, but that is the exception rather than the rule. The rule is considerate family planning together with even the children having a chance to make suggestions without being told to "Shut up, I didn't ask *you*."

And it is right at this point that most homes make a mistake as children grow older. We parents tend to keep on making decisions for our children when they, at twelve, sixteen, twenty, ought increasingly to be making decisions for themselves. As children show capacity to handle their own lives they should be gradually cut loose from the apron strings and set free in the world to stand or fall by their own choices. Only so will they learn self-reliance and private judgment and the difference between right and wrong.

The last important difference between a mere house and a real home is that in a home the ideals and dreams and hopes of a practical religion are always giving substance and stability to wavering tempers and drifting conduct. I don't see how any home can stand up long unless it is built on the rock of solid religion. Now mark you, I am not saying *what* religion, but behind every home, and underneath it, there should be the power and beauty and conscience and friendliness of a living religion. Without this your home becomes too self-centered, too much a matter of, "Me and my family, just us, nobody else." And that is too small a world for a day like this when our only hope is that the whole earth will soon become a family, helping each other instead of bombing each other. True, a home can drift along for a few years without religious anchorage, moving on the momentum of past fidelity to faith, but there comes a day when tragedy catches up with every family, and then it is that a strong and understanding religion becomes a necessity as an anchor for the soul. No home can live forever on grandmother's religion. St.

Peter does not let us in on the statement, "But my grandmother was a fine woman." He asks a very plain question, "What was the faith by which you—not your grandmother—lived?"

America is in the midst of a housing program. Let us put ourselves in the midst of a homing program.

THE LAVENDER MAN

SPEAKING of the usefulness of useless things, there is sweet lavender. "Sweet lavender, sweet lavender, five cents a package." For over twenty years the Lavender Man has sold lavender on his noisy corner. He stands near the curb with his old derby hat, black coat and his basket of lavender sachets. He tells me he makes a living out of the business, too. The lavender comes from Kent, England, where it is cut from the hedges just at the right ripeness of the blossoms. Then it is dried and broken into a fragrant mixture, sewn up into little bags. Stenographers at the State House like lavender for their handkerchiefs. Shopping wives take it home for the bureau drawers.

The lavender man is seventy-five years old come November and he is on his lavender corner, fair weather and foul. It has to be a very bad day to drive him in.

What did he do before he sold lavender? He was a circus barker with Hagenbeck and Ringling Brothers for fifty-three years. That must have meant a lot of talking. So his voice is quieter now. The newsboys outyell him, but they do not outsell him, with his quiet, "Sweet lavender, sweet lavender, five cents a package."

And he found his wife in the circus too. He married the girl on the flying trapeze, and they have lived happily ever after. Artie Wills is especially proud of his two bent fingers, broken when he was a catcher behind the bat in professional baseball.

In a world threatened with poison gas, I am glad for a man who sells sweet lavender. In a world of many kinds of bad smells, I am glad for a man who sells sweet lavender in the center of the city. In a world full of the smell of printer's ink I am glad for Artie Wills and his sweet lavender. In a world of gasoline fumes I am glad for Artie Wills and his sweet lavender. In a world of blackout and smoking ruins I am glad for Artie Wills and his sweet lavender.

In a world of subway trains I am glad for sweet lavender. In a world of whirling taxis I am glad for sweet lavender. In a world of politics and intrigue and communiqués I am glad for sweet lavender. In a world where there is axis and anti-axis I am glad for sweet lavender. In a world of ecumenical conferences and balances of power I am glad for "sweet lavender, sweet lavender, five cents a package." I think it would be cheap at ten times the price, just to have it around to remind us that there really is a world of sweetness and light and fragrance and delicacy and gentleness and aroma and nicety.

The usefulness of useless things? What is the use of a flower? Did it ever push a street car or win a war?

Yet a flower is as useful as anything on earth because it feeds the heart and elevates the mind and feasts the spirit.

It is at precisely this point that we are in genuine danger just now, we are in danger of becoming slaves to gadgets instead of devotees of lavender. We take a word like "gadget," and it becomes king, so that all the art and mystery and music of life vanish before the onslaught of this frankenstein, the gadget. So enslaved are we to making gadgets for a profit, so enslaved are we to using gadgets to cut all possible corners of moral and mental effort that we hardly understand the language of high romance and moral beauty and spiritual adventure.

I am asking that we save a little corner of our living for music and "sweet lavender, sweet lavender, five cents a package."

Here is the same idea in the words of Amiel:

"Let mystery have its place in you; do not be always turning up your whole soil with the plowshare of self-examination, but leave a little fallow corner of your heart ready for any seed the winds may bring, and reserve a nook of shadow for the passing bird; keep a place in your heart for the unexpected guest, an altar for the unknown God."

"Lavender, sweet lavender, five cents a package."

ART FOR PROFIT

AN ART SCHOOL not far away has this refreshingly frank caption near the front door, "Art for profit"!

Now I have often heard about "Art for art's sake," or "Art for pleasure," or "Art for a hobby," but never before have I seen it put so bluntly, "Art for profit."

I could see through the windows of that school that the classrooms are filled with attractive young women and handsome men, studying art for profit. That sign is pulling them in.

And why not? Even an artist likes to eat, and he cannot eat canvas. Nine out of ten artists find it impossible to practise their art for money enough to pay expenses, let alone for profit. Greenwich Village in the winter and Rockport in the summer overflow with artists who can provide a supply of really good pictures that is about a hundred times the size of the demand. But they go on painting, beause painting is in them, whether they get paid for it or not.

In many of our great cities, painters, musicians, poets, writers, by the boarding house full, are working at their art, and from what they tell me, and from what I see of their problems in holding body and soul together, I know this: if we are thinking of money returns, they are not practising art for profit, they are practising art for nothing. In times like these, when most people have all they can do to buy bread, maybe with butter, they are not likely to buy pictures. More likely we are to gather a boxful of family portraits from the attic and see what the seond-hand dealer will offer for them.

Art for profit? Yes, if you can get it in a world like this.

John Ruskin once described fine art as that in which the hand, the head and the heart go together. I like to think that the reason so few people ever make a profit out of art is because they put so much into it, hand, head, heart. They have the urge to create. That is paramount. If the created thing sells, so much the better, but it has to be made because it was in the soul of the artist. Then it gets into his heart as a deep emotion, a feeling for beauty. His head puts reasonableness into that emotion, brains temper it with form and texture. Then his hands, with exquisite skill, translate the emotion and the idea into color on canvas, form in stone, music in the voice or on the instrument. Such art is for soul expression, it is for a feast of beauty, for truth or for harmony. Such art is as necessary to the artist as the song is to the lark. But it is not for profit.

What I am trying to say is as old as the hills and as trite as a b c; we all have to make a living, but something is more important than making a living; that is, making a life. A living without a life is groceries in an empty house. But a life without a living may be a man starving for his convictions, starving for his high art which will not come down to popular levels of favor. No artist worthy of the name ever started out looking for a profit. He started out looking for a good idea to put into form. Maybe he never got paid for it, but he did not care much. Vincent Van Gogh was paid hardly enough for black bread and coffee in return for all his paintings. He needed a business manager badly. "Schubert sold his priceless songs for ten pence apiece but he did not write them for ten pence. Milton sold 'Paradise Lost' for ten pounds, but he did not write it for ten pounds," says Dr. Fosdick.

Whether we like it or not, we now have a world where the watchword of almost every profession is "What is there in it for me?"

Business for profit sounds quite right because we have always assumed that business was in business to make a profit. But now there is a public conscience which rises up and declares that business shall not make an excessive profit on the sweat of underpaid workers, nor on the idleness of laid-off workers.

Every business has a right to a profit, but when that profit comes by using false scales, or making life-preservers that will not float, or putting terra alba into children's candy, something is wrong. And what is wrong is that profit has been put first, when it should be second to integrity.

"Religion for profit." There is a new idea, although some kinds of religion have been run that way for a long time. When any church takes out of its people more than it gives them of courage and beauty and truth and God, that church should put a sign over its door, "Religion for profit."

"War for profit" is not the usual phrase, but that is what most war amounts to, profit for somebody and bloody loss for somebody else. We have sent bombs to Japan and bandages to China to soak up the blood the bombs spill. That is war for profit.

And among women who care for it, there is love for profit, too, but somebody pays too high a price for it.

But I am getting rather far afield. I began by talking about art, and that is the way I would like to close.

At 9 Harcourt Street, Boston, in a lofty barn-like workroom, we rediscovered the art of stained glass. Mr. Connick is just finishing the huge north window for a great church. He has set the window in a frame at one end of his loft so his friends can enjoy the color and symbolism and warmth of line in his latest creation. Here is a fine art if ever there was one, and there is not much profit in it. The other day I watched most of the forty-five helpers at their delicate work and this is what I saw:

First Mr. Connick, the master mind, outlines the window, deciding upon figures and symbols, after extensive research in heavy tomes of Christian history. Then a small-scale color drawing is made of the window. Then a full-scale drawing is made in black and white.

Glass comes to Mr. Connick from all over the world, in endless varieties of color and thickness and texture. I saw a bubbly glass which was made by putting potatoes in the boiling glass before it hardened.

Glass cutters then assemble and cut the various colors of glass to fit the pattern of the full-scale drawing. This glass is set in a bees wax frame and is then treated with paint for small details of design. After glazing in the oven to harden the paint, the glass is set in soft lead frames, then in larger steel frames which give the window strength to stand wind pressure.

Mr. Connick says that the process by which stained glass windows are made today is substantially the same as it was in the cathedral days of mediæval Europe. The principal change is that today electric ovens are used for glazing. In the olden days charcoal in earthen ovens did the work perfectly.

One window will often need as many as one thousand separate pieces of glass, each piece carefully cut to pattern. I stood in awe at the concentrated patience of these forty-five artists who help Mr. Connick create such unspeakable loveliness. No matter what you may or may not think of religion, few experiences of life can do as much for one's soul as to stand in a quiet church and watch the sun pour its light through a window whose color and form are a benediction and a melody of harmony to the spirit. No one of us is ever quite the same after an hour in such a place. I sometimes think such a window is better than a sermon, because it speaks the universal language of beauty, the thing the world is starved for just now. I pay my respects to Mr. Connick and his craftsmen who do get paid, I am sure, but who seemed interested in something else besides "Art for profit."

UNFINISHED SYMPHONY

WE AMERICANS have a passion for getting things done before the five o'clock whistle blows. We cannot bear the loose ends of unfinished business. "Get it done somehow," is the admonition behind us and before. "He never finishes anything he starts," is supposed to be the severest kind of condemnation. But it may be the mark of a man who starts things so big in their plan and so endless in their implications that they may never be finished.

For only little things ever get completely done, like paying the butcher and combing your hair, and when they are done they soon have to be done over again. Really worthwhile things seldom get finished as long as you live. When you meet someone who boasts that he always finishes everything he starts, ask him what he has started, then listen to the roll call of the minutiæ. A person of quality gets little things done quickly but the main power of his life is put into tasks too big to finish in one evening.

About 536 B.C. the children of Israel began to rebuild the fallen Temple at Jerusalem after their return from Babylon. The work progressed slowly, too slowly for a news commentator in the book of Ezra, who in 520 B.C. wrote, "From that time until now it has been rebuilding, and yet it is not finished." Now why should the vast temple be finished in sixteen years? Chartres, Rheims, Notre Dame Cathedrals, built in a later day, were not built in sixteen years. Several of the finest cathedrals are even yet unfinished after several centuries of building. It takes a long time to make something beautiful and enduring.

You can finish building a house but you can never finish building a home. If you are in a hurry for a house you can order one by mail and within a few weeks call in your friends for the housewarming. But homes are not built that way.

A home begins under a June moon with precious promises and unearthly dreams and the sweetest story ever told. Then, if things go smoothly after little preliminary quarrels, wedding bells ring out. One day a cradle to rock and, not long after, a school lunch to pack. Years later you walk into the office some fair morning and loudly proclaim, "Look at me, fellows, I am a grandfather." But where does it end? Some people break up their homes at Reno or some point in between. But they have not finished them, they have surrendered before finishing, they have quit in mid-flight, they have abandoned the fireside, for cause or for excuse. And if you counter that you know someone who has had to break up housekeeping, I will show you a little woman in a small room under the stairs who may have had to break up housekeeping, but she has not given up homekeeping, not by all the warm good cheer she manages to pack into that cubbyhole. She could say, "From that romantic day in June, even until now, my home has been building, and yet it is not finished." Believing that is the only way she can live.

You can finish learning your a b c's. You can never finish your education. The popularity of the adult education movement in America today, so well deserved, is a testimony to the conviction of the people that their education did not become complete upon graduation from school. When a young zoology student came to Professor Agassiz of Harvard, the wise teacher handed the young man a fish with these instructions, "Look at it carefully and draw what you see." In an hour the student returned with what he thought was a fair drawing. "You have hardly begun," said the teacher. "Take it back and look more carefully and draw what you see." To make a long story short, that student looked at that fish, inside and out, for one full college term, drawing what he saw. That is the secret of all genuine learning, the power to look at an object or an idea or a process until we know what we see, and know the meaning of what we see.

The sheer joy of pursuing a course of study on one's own is ineffable. No one has discovered the joy of the mind until he knows the self-propelling drive of a creative idea. Start with any healthy curiosity lying dormant in the brain. Wake it up and follow it wherever it leads, into familiar or unfamiliar territory. Be afraid of no superstition or tradition. Believe nothing because it has been believed before, but only because it proves true in current experience. Follow your idea in and out of the labyrinthine ways of your own and of other people's minds. Get the clearest answer you can to every question. Such a pursuit of learning will make you a self-determining personality and will save you from the chameleon mind which takes the color of its convictions from the surrounding milieu. What shall we say for the intellectual paucity of an age where a factory owner could boast that his workers "need have nothing on their minds"? Their thinking would be done for them. Or what of the level of creative thinking of an American driving public which was recently told in thousands of signs across the country, "Ask the dealer what to do, what to see, where to go." We are fast graduating into the kindergarten.

You can finish learning a set of manners. You never can finish building a character. Manners can be learned out of a book on etiquette. You can be coached as to which spoon to pick up first when you dine at the White House or how to bow when you are presented at the Court of St. James. But character can be learned only out of experience, personal and historic. And each new day brings some new test for your courage, your understanding, your gentleness, your integrity. Is there anyone who has attained a finished character? You do, however, hear of people with finished manners. Do manners make the man or woman? They help add a little polish to solid mahogany, to dependable character. But too high a polish on wood that is worm-eaten is misleading, to say the least.

Lord Chesterfield, famous for his letters of good advice written to his son, suggests in a letter from Dublin in 1745, "I desire you will particularly attend to the graceful motion of your arms; which, with the manner of putting on your hat, is all that a gentleman need attend to."

Is that all that a gentleman need attend to? Let it only be said that the subsequent personal history of Lord Chesterfield's son does not give convincing evidence that manners only will make a man.

But of our characters, let each of us be able to say humbly, "From that time when I began to take charge of my own life even until now I have been building a soul, and yet it is not finished."

You can finish learning the names of the books of the Bible. You never can finish your religion. We used to get a prize in Sunday School for racing through from Genesis to Revelation in fourteen seconds. But our religion cannot be done so swiftly. No religion is ever finished, perfect. Our personal religion must grow with our growing awareness of the meaning and the problems of life. "New occasions teach new duties, time makes ancient good uncouth." If your religion is exactly the same in every detail today as it was ten years ago, either something is wrong with you or something is wrong with your religion.

Indeed, your religion may be built on old, eternal truth, if you are sure it is truth and not humbug. But that religion will revise and repair itself and touch new horizons the older you grow. God is indeed the same yesterday, today and forever, but our comprehension of Him alters as science and philosophy and human experience and common sense move from primordial darkness into the half-light of dawn.

Once a small boy fell out of bed in his sleep. When his mother asked him what had happened, he answered with more truth than humor, "I guess I went to sleep too near the place where I got in." Thousands of people go to sleep too near the place where they get into their religion. They join a church and then think they are on the train to heaven with no chance of being put off this side of the pearly gates. From the dawn of history, even until now, true religion and undefiled has been building and yet it is not finished.

In other words, your life is an unfinished symphony. Some years ago a contest was held to complete Schubert's Unfinished Symphony, with hundreds of suggested completions submitted to the judges. Thanks be to common sense, all the proposed endings were discarded and the symphony was left unfinished.

Two of Leonardo da Vinci's finest pictures are his Adoration of the Magi in the Uffizi Galleries, Florence, and his St. Jerome in the Vatican. Both pictures are unfinished, left in basic brown and white without other colors. My friend, Ella Munsterburg, believes that da Vinci would have said he never finished any picture. Always he could have given a finer light to a face, a clearer line to a hand, a deeper clarity to a background. He never finished any picture.

So, if you complain that it is discouraging to be dealing in unfinished business, remember that it is better to have composed the Unfinished Symphony than to have completed the latest song-sheet ditty, finished, but so small in its completion. It is better to have painted an unfinished Adoration of the Magi than to have completed the cover on last month's comic magazine.

Your life, at its best, will always be an unfinished symphony.